INSIDE
CODING

**Everything you need to get started with
programming using Python**

New York

INSIDE
CODING

Everything you need to get started with programming using Python

Mike Saunders

New York

This edition published in 2019 by:
The Rosen Publishing Group, Inc.
29 East 21st Street
New York, NY 10010

Cataloging-in-Publication Data
Names: Saunders, Mike.
Title: Inside coding / Mike Saunders.
Description: New York : Rosen YA, 2019. | Series: The geek's guide to computer science | Includes glossary and index.
Identifiers: LCCN ISBN 9781508181132 (pbk.) | ISBN 9781508181101 (library bound)
Subjects: LCSH: Python (Computer program language)--Juvenile literature. | Computer programming--Juvenile literature.
Classification: LCC QA76.73.P98 S28 2019 | DDC 005.13'3--dc2

Manufactured in the United States of America

Originally published in English by Haynes Publishing under the title: Coding manual © Mike Saunders 2017

Cover: Patarapoom/Shutterstock.com

Contents

Introduction   6

01. Setting up   8
- How to install Python   11
- Writing and running programs   15
- What error messages mean   17

02. Python basics   18
- Printing text to the screen   20
- What are variables?   22
- Doing simple maths   24
- Getting input   25

03. Changing the flow   30
- The ifs and buts of Python   32
- More conditional statements   35
- Repetition with loops   38

04. Save time with functions   42
- Creating simple functions   44
- Passing parameters   47
- Variable scope   50
- Fun with built-in functions   51

05. Dealing with data   54
- What are data structures?   56
- The magic of tuples   57
- Lists and dictionaries   60
- Data and functions   67

06. Saving your results   70
- Saving data to files   72
- Reading text and binary   75
- Searching through files   79
- Handling Python data   82

07. Do more with modules   86
- What is a module?   88
- Bundled with Python   90
- Handy extra modules   95

08. A class of its own   102
- What are classes?   105
- Getters, setters and logic   107
- Inheritance   109
- Using slots   110

09. Sample programs   112
- Bat-and-ball game   114
- Employee directory   116
- Text editor   118
- Headlines   120

Challenge answers   122
Glossary   123
For More Information   124
For Further Reading   125
Index   126

INSIDE CODING
Introduction

Just a decade ago, the word "programming" had plenty of negative connotations. Most people would think of programmers as cubicle-dwelling wage slaves, who stare at their screens for eight hours a day, churning out incomprehensible gobbledygook. And what about people who took up programming as a hobby? That would be the domain of bearded geeks who play Dungeons and Dragons, right?

Today, that couldn't be further from the truth. Programming (or coding, or hacking, or whatever you want to call it) has become cool. People are waking up to the fact that it's not a black art, something that's completely out of reach for the masses. Children are coding, moms and dads are coding, retired people are coding – and doing fascinating work. Programmers talk about their career or hobby with pride, and not with fear that they'll be labelled as "that nerd."

But why is this? What has happened to change the perception so significantly? Well, we'd point to three key reasons. Firstly, some governments are starting to recognize the importance of coding in education. When this author was at school in the UK, back in the '80s and early '90s, IT was a purely optional subject that very few kids took up (and those who did were immediately labelled as geeks, as mentioned). Today, the UK government is really encouraging children to learn programming early on, and get into the right mindset for it, which in turn removes the stigma associated with it. After-school Code Clubs **(www.codeclub.org.uk)** have been storming successes.

Real-life skills
And this leads to the second reason for the upswing in coding's popularity: people are realizing that it teaches valuable skills. When you learn to program, you learn much more than a bunch of weird-looking words and symbols – you learn to think more logically, to compartmentalize things, to break them down to their subcomponents, and to think of new ways to approach problems. Learn how to code and you can tackle many daily challenges much more effectively.

Finally, a certain credit card-sized computer has done wonders for the popularity of programming. Millions of Raspberry Pis have been sold around the world, and while they can be used for a huge variety of tasks, they're especially well suited to programming. They're cheap, simple, can be plugged into a TV, and are equipped out-of-the-box with the Python programming language that's the subject of this book.

Why Python?
But what makes Python so special? Why have we chosen it to be the focus of this guide, when there are so many programming languages out there? In a nutshell, Python has everything. Compared to some languages which look cryptic and even menacing, Python code is easy to read and is closer to natural human language. If you've tried to learn coding before and been put off by all the weird symbols and constructs that some languages use, you'll feel right at home here.

At the same time, Python isn't just a language for new developers. It has been around for decades, and has been steadily refined and improved, with plenty of real-world use to back it up. Python is employed in everything from little scripts that sort text files right up to large graphical applications. Although the language itself is simple at its core, there are many bolt-on modules you can use to write more versatile and powerful programs – as we'll see in the later chapters of this book.

More and more children are getting into programming at an early age, thanks to after-school Code Clubs.

python™

This book focuses on the Python programming language, but the skills you learn will be transferable to other languages as well.

And the great thing about learning to code is: very few things in programming are really language-specific. Sure, different programming languages have different features and ways of doing things, but ultimately they all end up telling the CPU, the processor in your computer, what to do. Once you've gone through this book and have become an efficient and knowledgeable Python hacker, you can easily tackle other languages – and indeed, learning other languages is a great way to become an even better programmer.

The journey starts here

So you're about to begin your journey. You might be slightly intimidated by the road ahead, especially if you've flicked to some later pages in the book and glanced at the listings of Python code, but worry not. Everyone can learn how to code. This author has been teaching people how to do it for decades. It's one of the best things you can do, for your brain, for your way of thinking, for a new hobby, or even for a new career.

So let's get started!

01.
Setting up

In this section

How to install Python   11

Installing on Windows
Installing on macOS
Installing on Linux
Installing on Raspberry Pi

Writing and running programs   15

On Windows
On macOS
On Linux (including Raspberry Pi)

What error messages mean   17

Before we begin our programming adventure, you need to install the Python programming language onto your computer. If you're already familiar with your operating system, you may have noticed that Python is already installed – this is true in the case of macOS and most Linux distributions. However, the version of Python included with those operating systems is often old and out of date, and we want the latest and greatest.

Note that Python is completely free to use and share; it's open-source software, so anyone can look at the source code behind it (the human readable "recipe"), make changes and send them back to the developers. Indeed, by the end of this book, you may be interested in peeking under the hood of Python to see what makes it tick – and even add new features to the language! If you need it, the full license for Python is available online at: **www.python.org/psf/license/.**

If you're completely new to the world of free and open-source software, you may wonder why something

so powerful and widely used as Python is completely free. Don't the developers want to make money from it? Who does all the work on it without any financial reward? Well, in the open-source world it's typical for the core product to be free, and then developers make money by selling add-on solutions, documentation and support. Take Linux, for example: it's completely free to use and share, but companies like Canonical, Red Hat and Google (see Android) build upon it with paid-for features and support contracts, and they make plenty of money to put food on the tables of developers.

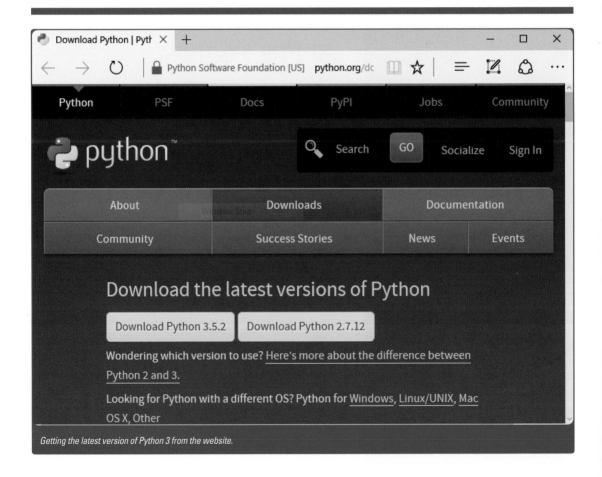

Getting the latest version of Python 3 from the website.

SETTING UP
How to install Python

Anyway, let's install Python. Because there are so many different versions of Windows, Linux and macOS out there, it's hard to cover absolutely every possibility in one section – not without taking up half of the book. So we'll cover the basics here, which will be fine for 99% of users, but if you happen to have a very custom setup and can't get it to work, you may have to do some more research about your operating system.

Installing on Windows

We're using Windows 10 in this case, but the process should be the same (or at least very similar) for other versions of Windows. In your web browser, go to **www.python.org/downloads/**, and click the yellow button that says "Download Python 3.x" (the .x will be followed by the most recent version number). We'll be using Python 3 throughout this book – so make sure that you get that version, and not Python 2, Python 4, or whatever else may have been released by the time you read this!

You'll then be redirected to a page listing various downloads for Windows. Scroll down to the Files section, and click on "Windows x86-64 executable installer" (if your CPU and Windows version is 64-bit, like most recent PCs) or "Windows x86 executable installer" (for older 32-bit PCs). Choose to save the file to your hard drive – it's around 30MB.

Once the download has finished, use Windows Explorer to navigate to the folder where it was saved (e.g. Downloads) and double-click the file. If you're prompted

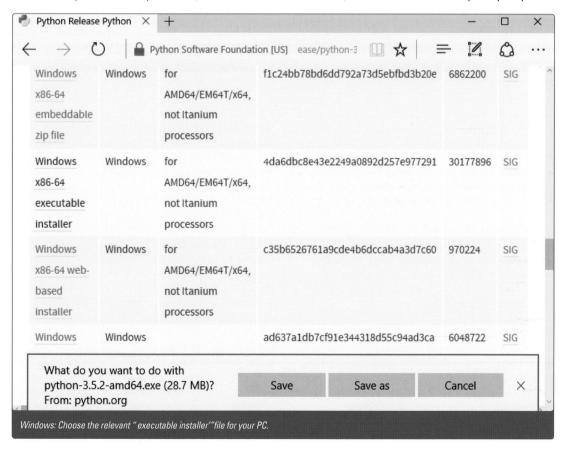

Windows: Choose the relevant " executable installer'"file for your PC.

Important! Check the "Add Python 3.x to PATH" box during installation.

for confirmation to run it, just click Run – then the installer window will appear.

Important: at the bottom of the installer screen is a checkbox saying "Add Python 3.x to PATH." You need to check this box to make sure you can run Python programs from the command line.

So with that box checked, click "Install Now" and the files will be copied onto your hard drive. When the installation has finished, click Close to exit the installer – and you're done! You can now delete the installer file you downloaded, and move on to the next section to learn how to run Python programs.

Installing on macOS
If you're using a Mac, you do have access to Python straight away – albeit a much older version (usually 2.7). In this book we're using Python 3, which is a more modern release with many useful features, so you'll need to install that version manually. It's not a big job, though.

First of all, go to **www.python.org/downloads/** in your browser – you should see buttons offering you

the latest version for macOS. Click the button that says "Download Python 3," which will then start a download of a .pkg file of around 25MB. Once the download has finished, locate the .pkg file in Finder (e.g. in your Downloads folder) and double-click it to start the installation process.

Click "Continue" to display some technical release notes; you don't need to be concerned with these for now, so just click "Continue" again and then confirm that you agree with the license (as mentioned, Python is open source and free for all to use). Then click "Install" to copy the files to your hard drive – you may be asked for your password at this point. After a few moments, Python 3 will be installed on your system and you can close the installer window and delete the .pkg file you downloaded.

Installing on Linux
Good news for Linux users: Python 3 is installed by default in virtually every major Linux distribution released in the last few years. To check this, open a command line window – typically known as Terminal, XTerm or Konsole depending on the desktop environment you have installed (it should be somewhere in your program menu).

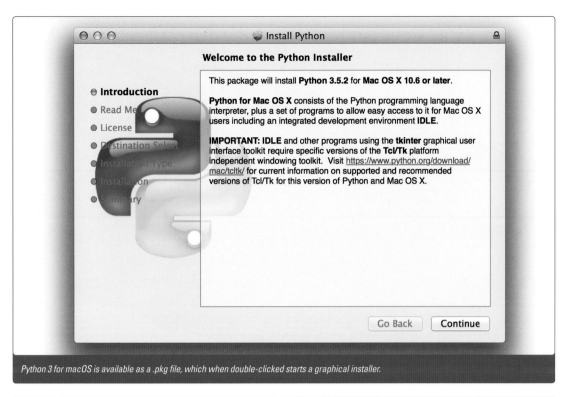

Python 3 for macOS is available as a .pkg file, which when double-clicked starts a graphical installer.

Once you've agreed to the open-source license, Python 3 will be copied to your hard drive and is then ready to use.

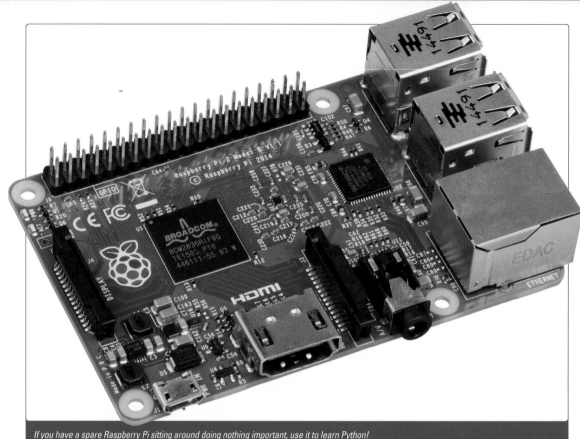

If you have a spare Raspberry Pi sitting around doing nothing important, use it to learn Python!

Now, at the command prompt, enter "python3" and see what happens. All being well, you'll see a message stating the full version number, like this:

```
Python 3.4.2 (default, Oct 19 2014, 13:31:11)
[GCC 4.9.1] on linux
Type "help", "copyright", "credits" or "license" for more ↵
  information.
>>>
```

Congratulations, you're ready for Python! The ">>>" part is a prompt for you to start entering Python instructions – but we don't need that for the moment. Press Ctrl+D to exit Python and return to the command prompt, where you can close the window.

If you don't see the above message, but receive an error message instead, it means that Python 3 isn't installed. Every Linux distribution has its own way of installing software, so try looking in your package manager for Python 3 and installing it. If you still have trouble, try searching on your distribution's website or asking a question on the very useful forums at **www.linuxquestions.org/questions/**.

Installing on Raspberry Pi

The Raspberry Pi makes for a great little Python development box. Raspbian, the most commonly used Linux distribution on the Pi, is constantly being updated so it may include Python 3 by the time you read this – so just try to run it by entering "python3" as in the general instructions for Linux provided before. If you're using an older version of Raspbian with Python 2, you can install the newer version by entering the following command in a terminal window:

```
sudo apt-get install python3
```

You will be prompted for your password, and then the Python 3 packages will be downloaded from the internet. You can then enter "python3" to check that it has installed correctly.

SETTING UP
Writing and running programs

So, you're almost ready to begin learning Python. But for the rest of this book, we want to concentrate entirely on the programming language itself, and not on the little differences between operating systems. So here we'll quickly show you the methods for writing and running Python programs, which you can then use as you start to master the language.

One important thing to note from the start is: Python programs are written in plain text. So you need to use a plain text editor when writing code – not a word processor, or a web editor, or anything like that. A simple text editor that normally saves files in .txt format is ideal.

On Windows

For beginner programmers, the best tool for writing Python code is the venerable Notepad text editor, included with every version of Windows going back to version 1.0 in 1985. You'll find it in your program menu or via the search bar in newer Windows versions, so start it up and then enter the following text:

```
print("Test")
```

This is a very (very!) simple Python program that prints the word "Test" on the screen. Save this file onto your desktop as "test.py" (without a .txt extension). Next, open up a

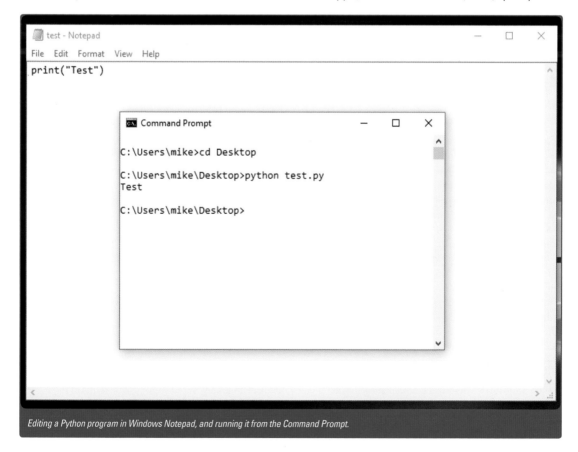

Editing a Python program in Windows Notepad, and running it from the Command Prompt.

Editing a Python program in macOS TextEdit, and running it from the Terminal.

Apple's macOS includes a simple but decent text editor that we can use for writing Python programs – and it's called, funnily enough, TextEdit. Launch it from Finder (it's in the Applications folder) or via Spotlight, and enter the following text:

```
print("Test")
```

Now, Python programs must be saved in plain text, but your version of TextEdit may be configured to use fancy formatting and other features that we don't need. In the menu, go to Format and see if there's an option near the top called Make Plain Text – and if so, click it. This should remove the formatting toolbar so all you see is raw text, which is exactly what we want. (And to avoid having to do this for each Python program you write, go to TextEdit > Preferences in the menu, and then select "Plain text" under the Format options at the top.)

Next, save the file as test.py (no .txt extension) onto your Desktop. Then open Terminal from the Applications folder (inside Utilities) or via Spotlight, which lets us use the macOS command line. Enter the following commands:

```
cd Desktop
python3 test.py
```

This switches your current location ("cd" means "change directory") to the folder of the macOS desktop, and then runs Python 3, telling it to execute the contents of the "test. py" file we saved beforehand. If you want to execute a different Python program in the future, just change the file name accordingly. All being well, you'll see results like in the screenshot.

Command Prompt – also available in the program menu or via the search bar – and enter the following commands:

```
cd desktop
python test.py
```

This switches your current location ("cd" means "change directory") to the directory for the Windows desktop, and then runs Python, telling it to execute the contents of the "test.py" file we saved beforehand. If you want to execute a different Python program in the future, just change the file name accordingly. All being well, you'll see results like in the screenshot – "Test" should be displayed in the Command Prompt window.

Note that you can keep Notepad open for editing your "test.py" file, and the Command Prompt window also open, so that you can keep running your program every time you save it. In the Command Prompt, you can also press the up arrow key to re-show the previously entered command, so that you can re-use it without having to manually enter "python test.py" every time.

If you have a problem, you may have missed the "Add Python 3.x to PATH" checkbox during installation, so uninstall Python and reinstall it, following the steps provided earlier.

On Linux (including Raspberry Pi)

Linux distributions vary enormously in terms of the programs included and desktop environments available, so we can't go into specifics here. But the two things you need are: access to a text editor, and access to the command line (usually via a program known as the Terminal). You should be able to find both of them in your program menu. In the text editor, create a file with the following contents:

```
print("Test")
```

Save this as "test.py" on your desktop. Then open a terminal window and enter the following:

```
cd Desktop
python3 test.py
```

All being well, the word "Test" should appear. If not, you may need guidance for your specific Linux distribution, so try your distro's website or ask a question on **www.linuxquestions.org/questions/** to get help.

The process is similar on a Raspberry Pi in desktop mode – but if you're accessing your Pi over the network via SSH, you can use the Nano text editor to write and save programs. To learn how to use Nano, search the web for a guide – there's a good one at **http://tinyurl.com/7djaprl**.

 Text editor options

We've covered the no-frills text editors included by default with operating systems here, but as your Python skills develop, you may want to investigate other editors with more advanced features. These include syntax highlighting (so your code looks colorful and easier to read, like in the listings in this book), auto-completion (so you don't have to type full commands each time) and other goodies.

For Windows users, we recommend Notepad++ (**https://notepad-plus-plus.org**), a free and open-source editor designed for programmers. If you're using a Mac, some options include Sublime Text (**www.sublimetext.com**) and SlickEdit (**www. slickedit.com**). And on Linux, the two most popular advanced editors are Emacs and Vim – you'll find them in your package manager. They take a while to learn, so you'll have to consult some online tutorials, but the results are worth it!

SETTING UP
What error messages mean

So now you're set up to write, save and run Python programs. But before we get into the coding, let's look at a few common error messages so you know how to deal with them in the future. Firstly:

```
can't open file 'test.py': [Errno 2] No such file ↵
   or directory
```

This simply means that Python cannot find the file that you specified – in this case, "test.py". Either you haven't saved "test.py" anywhere, or the file has a different name like "test.py.txt", or you are not running Python in the same directory as where you saved it. (Remember the "cd" command earlier, to switch into the same place where the "test.py" file is.)

If you're struggling to get into the directory where you saved your file, try searching the web for an introduction to the command line for your specific operating system.

Ultimately, though, you should only need the "cd" command to move around before running Python.

```
SyntaxError: unexpected character after line ↵
   continuation character
```

In this case, you may have not saved your Python program as plain (ASCII) text, but rather a specific word processor format such as Rich Text Format or an office suite format. Always make sure that your Python programs are stored as plain text.

```
can't open file 'test.py': [Errno 13] Permission denied
```

This should very rarely happen, but if it does, you don't have read access to the "test.py" file that you created. You will need to use your operating system's file manager to enable read access for the user you're logged in as – see your operating system's documentation for details.

02.
Python
basics

In this section

Printing text to the screen   20
Putting it all together

What are variables?   22
When two become one

Doing simple math   24
Remain seated

Getting input   25
Strings and numbers
A function in a function

Challenge yourself   29

With your editor and command prompt set up, your fingers are no doubt itching to start programming. And in this book, we're going to focus on the practical side of coding – actually getting things done. Of course, you'll learn a lot of theory and background along the way, but in contrast to dusty old textbooks (like you may have seen at school), we won't spend page after page explaining abstract concepts before looking at real code.

No, the best way to learn is by actually doing. So as we progress through the book, we'll look at code samples first, give you time to explore them and try them out, and then go through them in detail so that you're fully familiar with what's happening.

It's also a good idea to play around with the code samples yourself – try changing bits, rearranging lines and so forth. The worst that can happen is that your Python program simply won't run! So let's get started.

PYTHON BASICS
Printing text to the screen

Here's your first Python program – well, strictly speaking it's not quite the first, as you wrote one earlier to test your Python installation. But here's where the real programming begins:

LISTING 1:

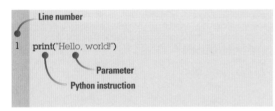

There is one thing to note about the formatting here: on the left-hand side are line numbers, which you shouldn't insert into your Python code – we only use them throughout this book for reference. So all you need is the line starting with "print" and ending with the closing bracket.

Now let's get back to the code itself: Listing 1 is a simple program that prints some text to the screen. Save it into your "test.py" file and run it, and as expected, "Hello, world" appears on the screen. But what exactly is going on here? What is the process that occurs, from us typing things into a text editor to words appearing on the screen?

Well, when we run Python with the "test.py" file, the Python interpreter starts up and looks at the contents of the file. We call it an interpreter as it scans through the human-readable source-code file, works out what we're trying to do, and then tells the operating system what needs to be done. If we wanted to talk to the operating system – or even the hardware – directly, in order to put text on the screen, it would be immensely complicated. But Python does all the hard work for us.

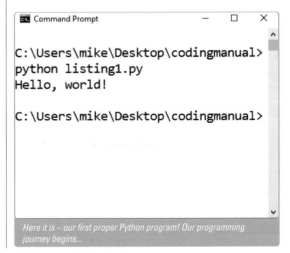

Here it is – our first proper Python program! Our programming journey begins...

Putting it all together

So our program here has two parts: a Python command, called "print", and a parameter which is a piece of information that we supply with the "print" command. The brackets are there to show exactly what information is part of the print command – without them, we may not be sure exactly which bits of text belong to which command.

So here we say to Python: we want you to print something, and the thing to print is inside the brackets. Note that we use quotation marks to say that we want to print an exact line or "string" of text, verbatim – if we remove the quotation marks, it has a very different meaning. More on that in a moment.

In Python, each command goes on its own line. And you can add as many commands as you want. So for instance, we could separate the above program into two parts:

 Tip

You may wonder why the command is "print", rather than something more sensible like "display". After all, we're not printing anything out! Well, it's mostly historical – many programming languages that inspired Python came to life in the 1960s and 1970s, when graphical monitors weren't so common, and developers used old-style teletype devices that physically printed text on to paper rolls. How far we've come...

LISTING 2:

```
1   print("Hello,")
2   print("world!")
```

There – we've just doubled the length of the program! But each word is printed on a separate line now. We'll deal with that later.

PYTHON BASICS
What are variables?

By far the most useful and important element of programming is the variable. As the name suggests, this is something that can vary – but that doesn't really say a lot. Put simply, a variable is a storage space in the computer's memory that we can use for things that change often. For example, consider your wallet or purse, and specifically the amount of money inside it. We could describe your wallet or purse as a variable, saying it sometimes has $20, or maybe $200 (on a good day). The amount varies inside, but the storage space – the physical wallet or purse – always remains the same.

Now let's see how this works in Python:

LISTING 3:

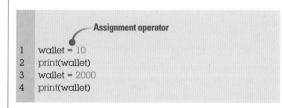
Assignment operator

```
1    wallet = 10
2    print(wallet)
3    wallet = 2000
4    print(wallet)
```

In line 1 of Listing 3, we create a new variable – a new storage space in the computer's memory – called "wallet". In the same line, using the equals (=) sign, which is also

known as the assignment operator, we tell Python that "wallet" should store the number 10. Following that, in line 2, we then use our now-familiar "print" command to display the contents of the "wallet" variable on the screen.

But wait! This time we're not using any quotation marks. Why is that? Well, we are not printing a specific line of text this time – we don't actually want to print the word "wallet" to the screen. (If we wanted to do that, we would use the quotation marks like we did earlier.) No, we want to print what's inside our "wallet" variable, so we put the variable name on its own.

So, line 2 displays the number 10 on the screen. In line 3, we see that it's possible to keep using variables after they have been created. As far as we're concerned, the "wallet" variable remains available until the program ends – so we can use it to store other numbers. In line 3, we update "wallet" to contain a bigger number now, 2000. And then in line 4, we print that number to the screen.

Tip

When you create variables, you can give them almost any names, with a few restrictions: they must start with a letter (and not a number), and they must not clash with any other instructions and keywords used in Python. You can't, for instance, create a variable called "print" because that is already used for displaying text.

When two become one

Earlier we talked about the importance of brackets when using Python commands, to show which bits of information belong to a specific command. Look at the program in Listing 4:

LISTING 4:

```
1   wallet = 10
2   purse = 50
3   print(wallet, purse)
```

Here you can see that we create two new variables called "wallet" and "purse", and then tell them to store the numbers 10 and 50 respectively. In line 3, we provide multiple parameters – bits of information – to Python's "print" command. We separate these with commas, and

Python then displays "10 50" on the screen when we run the program. As you'll see throughout this book, we often provide lots of information to commands, all placed neatly into brackets and separated by commas.

So far we've just been placing numbers into our variables, but it's also possible to put pieces of text – known as strings – into them as well. This is where the quotation marks come in to play again. What do you think happens in Listing 5?

LISTING 5:

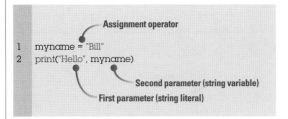

Here we tell Python to create a new variable called "myname", and tell it to store the text string "Bill". If we didn't use quotation marks here, Python would get confused, thinking that "Bill" is actually another variable that we haven't used yet. But by providing quotation marks, it's clear that we want the exact text string "Bill" to be stored. Such a string is often known as a "string literal".

Then, in line 2, we tell the "print" command to display two things: a text string that says "Hello", followed by the contents of our "myname" variable. So the result is "Hello Bill" as seen in the screenshot. (Python adds a space to the end of "Hello" – but more on that later.)

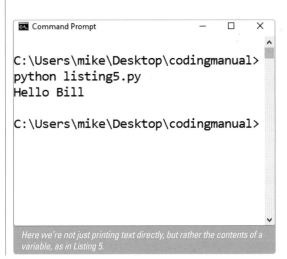

Here we're not just printing text directly, but rather the contents of a variable, as in Listing 5.

PYTHON BASICS
Doing simple math

So far we've used numerical variables like "wallet" and "purse", along with a string variable in the form of "myname". But up to this point, we haven't really done any varying with them – we haven't actually made much use of them as variables. We've just pushed some data into them and that's it. But variables really come to life when you start manipulating them – for example, using mathematical operations. Look at Listing 6:

LISTING 6:

```
1  a = 10
2  b = 5
3  c = a + b
4  print(c)
```

You may have already guessed what happens here, but just to be clear: we create two new numerical variables, called "a" and "b", and store the numbers 10 and 5 in them respectively. Next, we create another numerical variable called "c", to which we assign "a" added to "b" (using the plus sign). Then we display the contents of "c" on the screen – so 15 in this case.

Tip

As you write more elaborate programs, it's important to give variables useful names, like "wallet" mentioned earlier. This helps if you write a lot of code and come back to it later, when you may need to reread it to work out what it does. But for short programs where variables are just used for testing, it's fine to use names like "a" and "b", like in Listing 6.

Python has many other mathematical operations as well, along with the plus one we've just looked at. For instance, you could replace line 3 in Listing 6 with all the variants in Listing 7:

LISTING 7:

```
1  c = a - b
2  c = a * b
3  c = a / b
4  c = a % b
```

Line 1 here is a subtraction (minus) operation, so the result of 10 minus 5 is, of course, 5. Line 2 uses the asterisk character – usually generated with Shift+8 on your keyboard – to perform multiplication, with the result being 50. Line 3 uses a forward slash which represents division, so the result of 10 divided by 5 is 2.

Remain seated

The final line in Listing 7, using the percentage (%) operator, is a bit special. This performs a modulo operation to find the remainder after a division. To see it in action, edit the first line in Listing 6 so that the variable "a" takes on the value 13 rather than 10. Then use the modulo (%) operator in line 3, run the program and see the result. What happens?

Well, the answer this time is 3. This is because the modulo operation finds the remainder after performing a division. When we perform 13 modulo 5, we get a quotient of 2 (because two 5s fits into 13) and a remainder of 3. Note that it's possible to bunch multiple math operations together, but be careful with the order:

LISTING 8:

```
1  a = 10
2  b = 5
3  c = 3
4  d = a + b * c
5  print(d)
```

What would you guess is the result of the math done in line 4 – what gets stored in the "d" variable? You may be tempted to say 45, which would make sense – after all, if you add "a" to "b", you get 15, and if you multiply that by "c" (3), you get 45. But hold on a minute! When you run the program, you'll see that line 5 prints out 25 instead.

This is due to something called "operator precedence." It's not something we have to concern ourselves with here, but it basically says that multiplication operations are more important than (or take precedence over) addition operations. So in line 4, Python decides to do the "b * c" multiplication operation first, resulting in 15, which is then added to the 10 in "a". Hence the result of 25.

To fix this, and to make the program clearer, we can place the first operation inside brackets, like so:

LISTING 9:

```
4    d = (a + b) * c
```

This makes it very clear – both to us, and to the Python interpreter – that only the results of "a" added to "b" should then be multiplied by "c". So we get 45.

If you want to add raw numbers to a variable, there are a couple of ways to do it, like in Listing 10:

LISTING 10:

```
1    a = 10
2    a = a + 5
3    a += 5
                    Does the same as in line 2
4    print(a)
```

Lines 2 and 3 do the same thing here: they take the contents of "a" and add 5 to it. (Line 3 is just a shorthand version of line 2.) So they're essentially saying: "a" should now contain whatever's already stored in "a", but with another 5 added on top. You can use the shorthand version with other math operators as well, e.g. "a -= 5" to subtract 5 from whatever's stored in "a".

PYTHON BASICS
Getting input

Almost every program of any significance will involve some kind of input from the user. This could be via keyboard presses, or mouse movements, or joystick movements. Unless you just want to draw pretty pictures on the screen, you'll need to involve the user in some way, so let's look at our options.

Python is equipped with various instructions we can use for displaying and inputting text. We've already seen one, "print", and its counterpart for retrieving information from the user is the aptly named "input".

Note that in programming parlance, the technical term for these instructions is "functions" – because they're a lot more powerful and versatile than simple instructions. We've already seen that you can use multiple parameters (pieces of data) with the "print" function, for instance, like in Listing 5. (We will look at functions in more detail later in the book, including how to make your own.)

Anyway, back to input: let's say we want to get the user's name, and then print a welcome message back to him or her, using that name. We use Python's built-in "input" function like so:

LISTING 11:

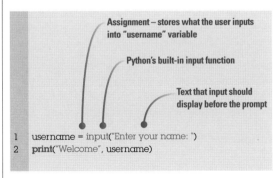

Assignment – stores what the user inputs into "username" variable

Python's built-in input function

Text that input should display before the prompt

```
1    username = input("Enter your name: ")
2    print("Welcome", username)
```

Here we have the first example of a Python function sending data back to us. Previously, when we were using "print", we were just telling it what to do – we didn't require anything back from it. But in this case, with "input", we actually want to save the words that the user types somewhere. And a variable is the perfect place to do that.

So in Listing 11, we create a new text variable called username, and then assign to it the results of the "input" function. This input function takes a parameter, which is a piece of text to be displayed before the prompt to type something in. So we tell Python's "input" function to display "Enter your name" on the screen, and then "input" waits for the user to type something and hit the Enter key.

Following that, whatever the user typed is stored in the "username" variable, and the program moves on to line 2. In that line, we print a piece of text followed by the contents of the "username" variable, in a similar fashion to before.

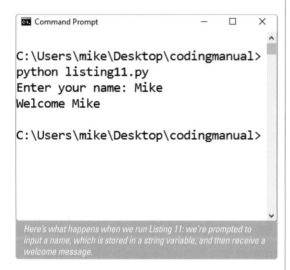

Here's what happens when we run Listing 11: we're prompted to input a name, which is stored in a string variable, and then receive a welcome message.

Strings and numbers

Of course, you can use multiple "input" functions in your code and print the results together – like in Listing 12, where we ask for the user's first name and last name separately, and then print them together:

LISTING 12:

```
1   firstname = input("Enter your first name: ")
2   lastname = input("Enter your last name: ")
3   print("Welcome", firstname, lastname)
```

It's worth remembering that variables are temporary storage spaces, and can be used again and again. As your programs become longer and more complicated, you may want to reuse variables to save memory.

 Tip

When you use the "print" function, and you put commas between the pieces of data (the parameters), Python automatically puts a space between them when displaying them on the screen – like in Listing 12. If you don't want that, replace the commas with plus (+) symbols – so "firstname, lastname" becomes "firstname+lastname". This displays the data exactly as it is, without any extra formatting.

For example, you might have a text variable called "tmp_string" (temporary string) that you use to store input before doing something else with it. Once the job is done, you can use "tmp_string" elsewhere in your program, without creating new variables each time. This can make your programs easier to read, and it means Python has fewer bits and bobs to keep track of as well.

Back to input: so far we've been working with text strings, like names, and Python's built-in "input" function does a great job here. But what happens if we want to use numbers? What do you think is the problem with Listing 13?

LISTING 13:

```
1   a = input("Enter a number: ")
2   b = input("And another: ")
3   print("The sum is", a + b)
```

This looks like it should make sense. In lines 1 and 2, we ask the user to input numbers. We store them in the "a" and "b" variables respectively. In line 3, we use the "print" function to display a message along with the sum of "a" and "b". But try it – enter 10 at the first prompt, and 20 at the second. The message you'll see is "The sum is 1020". That's not right at all! What's going on here? Have we found a bug in Python?

Well, no. This is all because Python still thinks we're working with strings of text. When we enter "10" and "20", Python doesn't see those as actual numbers, but instead treats them as sequences of key presses or letters – so the letter "1" followed by the letter "0", or "2" followed by "0". Python is simply joining the strings together – which is useful in some cases but not in others.

In order for Python to know we're working with real, specific numbers, we need to convert the results from the "input" function. And Python has a dedicated function to convert called "int":

LISTING 14:

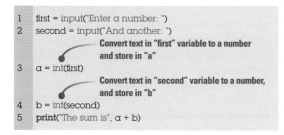

```
1    first = input("Enter a number: ")
2    second = input("And another: ")
                    Convert text in "first" variable to a number
                    and store in "a"
3    a = int(first)
                    Convert text in "second" variable to a number,
                    and store in "b"
4    b = int(second)
5    print("The sum is", a + b)
```

Here we ask the user to input two numbers, and store them in the "first" and "second" variables. At this point, Python doesn't know (or care) about the type of data we've entered – it's just assuming everything is a text string so far. To fix this, we use the "int" function, which takes one parameter, a text string variable, and returns (sends back) a proper number. So in lines 3 and 4, we create two new variables called "a" and "b", which are assigned the real numerical values contained in the "first" and "second" string variables respectively.

So when you run the program in listing 14, those two extra "int" functions in lines 3 and 4 do the job of converting

Tip

What is this "int" – what does it mean? It's short for "integer," which is the mathematical term used to describe a whole number. Integers can be positive and negative numbers, without decimal places, so they can be used in places where you don't need superfine levels of detail. Take ages or dates, for instance – you don't say you're 42.3 years old, or it's the 12.8th of March. In these cases, whole integer numbers do the trick.

text strings into proper numbers. Then, in the "print" function in line 5, we get the results of a real mathematical operation, and not just two text strings shoved next to each other.

Another type of number that's commonly used is floating point. This is like an integer but has digits after a decimal point – e.g. 3.14159. You can use these in Python as well, but you need to make it clear to Python. In Listing 14, for instance, you would change the "int" parts of lines 3 and 4 to be "float" instead, and then you can use numbers with decimal places.

A function in a function

Up until this point we've been using functions on their own – "print", "input" and "int", supplying parameters to them and sometimes getting bits of data back. But it's actually possible to feed the results of one function directly into another – obviating the need for additional variables in the middle.

For instance, look back at Listing 14: wouldn't it be great if we could immediately convert the results of the "input" functions in lines 1 and 2 into numbers, instead of having to create the extra "a" and "b" variables to store them? Well yes, that's certainly possible, like in Listing 15:

LISTING 15:

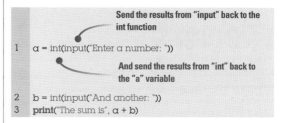

```
                           Send the results from "input" back to the
                           int function
1    a = int(input("Enter a number: "))
                           And send the results from "int" back to
                           the "a" variable
2    b = int(input("And another: "))
3    print("The sum is", a + b)
```

This is our most complicated program yet, and may look a bit baffling with all the brackets in various places. But to be clear how it works, let's go through line 1 – and from right to left, as that's how Python processes it.

The first thing Python runs is the "input" function with the text string we specify. But instead of assigning the result of "input" directly to a variable, as in Listing 14, we pass it directly into another function, "int". So you can see

Listing 15 shows how to convert multiple string inputs into integer numbers, and display the sum of them.

with the double brackets at the end of the line that we have effectively wrapped the "int" function around the "input" function. We are using two functions together here – hence the two closing brackets at the end of the line.

So "int" processes the results of "input", converting the text string into an integer number. Then we store the results of this "int" function in our variable "a". We repeat the process for the second number in line 2, and then print the sum in line 3 as usual. Et voila – the program in Listing 15 is shorter and more elegant than in Listing 14, and means we don't need to create extra variables to handle the transition between strings and numbers.

Feeding the results of one function into another is common practice in Python, and indeed most other programming languages, so it's a very useful technique to learn. Like with a foreign (human) language, it might require you to change your way of thinking early on, but you'll soon get used to it.

 Tip

If you're getting errors when trying to run programs where you're combining functions like in Listing 15, make sure you're using the right number of brackets. For instance, if you have two opening brackets in a line, there should be two closing brackets somewhere in the line as well. Even experienced programmers can sometimes forget to close a line with the right number of brackets, so if you see errors, it's worth checking for this first!

 Commenting your code

In this book we're using arrows and explanations to describe what's happening in the code listings. But as you write your own programs, you may want to leave your own notes and ideas, so that you can return to them later and understand what you meant when you wrote the code.

In programming lingo, such notes – which have no impact on how the program runs – are known as "comments," and Python completely ignores them.

For instance, let's take line 3 from Listing 14:

```
a = int(first)
```

This is a simple piece of code, but let's imagine we want to add a comment here to remind us what it does, when we return to it later. We do this using the hash (#) symbol like so:

```
a = int(first) # Convert "first" to a number
```

As soon as Python sees the hash symbol, it ignores the rest of the text up until the end of the line. Then it processes the following line as usual. You can place a comment next to a piece of code as in the above example; if you have a lot more to say, however, it's worth putting comments on their own lines, to describe the code that follows.

Comments are not only useful to document your code as you write it, so that you can understand it if you come back to it after a few months, but also for others as well. If you're writing a bigger program and want to share your Python code with other people, to get improvements or bug fixes, good comments will help those others to understand what you're doing. Don't just describe what you're doing but also why you're doing it!

? CHALLENGE YOURSELF

At the end of each section in this book, we'll pose you a few questions so that you can check that you've understood everything correctly. If you're in doubt, just turn back to the appropriate subsection and give it another read! You'll find all the answers in the "Challenge answers" section in the back of this book.

1. What restrictions do variable names have?
2. If variable "a" is a text string containing "123", how would you convert it to a real number and store it in variable "b"?
3. What is a floating-point number?
4. What is a shorthand way of saying "a = a + 5"?
5. How does Python interpret "10 + 5 * 3"?

03.
Changing the flow

In this section

The ifs and buts of Python   32
Our first code block
Multiple comparisons
More, less, equal to, or not?

More conditional statements   35
Alternatives to if: elif and else

Repetition with loops   38
The "while" loop
Checks and loops within loops
Infinite loops and breaking out
For loops

Challenge yourself   41

At this point, you know how to write and run Python programs with various features: displaying text on the screen, getting input from the user, working with variables and performing mathematical operations. These are vitally important first steps on your programming journey, but now we come to a new phase: changing how a program works, based on the contents of variables.

This allows us to create much more flexible programs than the ones we've written so far, which have been merely sequences of instructions for the Python interpreter to follow. In this section you'll learn how to jump to different parts of a program depending on various "conditions," so that you can do more interesting things with user input. You'll also learn how to automatically repeat entire sets of instructions – making Python do all the grunt work for you!

The ifs and buts of Python

Life is full of ifs. If the weather is good, I'll go for a walk. If I have enough money, I'll buy a shiny new laptop. If I learn Python, I'll try to develop a career as a programmer. These are all "conditions" – states of something or circumstances on which we then act. Indeed, we often bundle together multiple conditions in our daily lives: if the weather is good, I'll go for a walk; and on that walk, if I have enough money with me, I'll buy an ice cream.

It's exactly the same in programming: Python (and most other languages) make extensive use of "if" instructions to decide what to do. Let's see this in action, in Listing 16:

This short program introduces a bunch of new concepts, so let's go through them. You already know what line 1 does: it creates a new variable called "a" and places the number 1 inside it. Line 2 is blank (see the tip box for an explanation), and then on line 3 we meet Python's "if" instruction for the first time.

Now, you can probably work out what's going on here: we check to see if the contents of the "a" variable are equal to the number 2. But why do we have two equals signs?

LISTING 16:

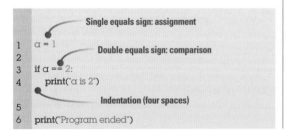

```
1   a = 1
2
3   if a == 2:
4       print("a is 2")
5
6   print("Program ended")
```

Single equals sign: assignment

Double equals sign: comparison

Indentation (four spaces)

Tip

In Listing 16, you'll notice that line 2 is blank – so what's the purpose of that? It doesn't have any effect on the program but is merely blank to help break up the different sections of code. It's always a good idea to put blank lines around "if sections (and code loops as we'll see later) to keep things clear and distinguish them from other chunks of code.

Can't we just use a single one like in line 1? Well, no. You see, the single equals sign always means an assignment – placing a number or text string into a variable.

If we used a single equals sign on line 3, it wouldn't be clear whether we're trying to perform an assignment (put the number 2 into "a") or perform a comparison. Indeed, with a single equals sign, Python could think, "Ah, this 'if' line is checking to see if the assignment works." And Python will be unsure and show an error message.

Our first code block

So whenever we perform a comparison, checking to see if the variable on the left matches the number or string on the right, we always use two equals signs. We end the "if" line with a colon (:) character, which tells Python to get ready for a new bunch of code (aka a "code block") that should only be run if the "if" condition is true.

But we have to be careful: in order to tell Python which code belongs to this specific "if" condition, we use indentation – moving the code slightly to the right. This makes it more readable for us, and makes it clear to

Indentation: tabs vs spaces

We use four spaces to indent code in this book, as that's the style recommended by the developers of Python. But some coders prefer to use tabs instead, which are typically eight spaces wide in most text editors. If you'd much rather use tabs in your programs, that's fine, but the most important thing is to stay consistent! Don't try to mix combinations of tabs and spaces inside a single code block.

On a related note, coding style is a hotly debated issue not just across Python but many other programming languages. Should you use capital letters in variable names? Should you break up long comments across multiple lines? How long should lines of code be before they become unwieldy? For the official Python stance on these questions (and others), see the Style Guide for Python Code at **www.python.org/dev/peps/pep-0008/**. It covers a lot of topics we haven't looked at yet, but it's worth bookmarking for later reference.

Python which bits of code belong where. So on line 4, we precede our "print" instruction with four spaces, and this line will only be run if "a" contains the number 2.

On line 6, we have a separate "print" instruction, but because this has not been indented with spaces, and isn't part of the code block belonging to the "if", Python will always execute it. So try running the program – it will just display the text on line 6. Then edit line 1 so that "a" starts off containing the number 2, and run it again; this time the "print" instruction in line 4 will be executed as well.

Multiple comparisons

In the previous program we compared a variable with a numerical value, but it's also possible to compare strings as well. On top of that, we can put one "if" code block inside another. Both of these features are demonstrated in Listing 17:

LISTING 17:

```
1   a = 2
2   name = "Bob"
3
4   if a == 2:
5       print("a is 2")
6       if name == "Bob":
```
                        Nested if statement
```
7           print("And name is Bob")
```
                        Double indentation (eight spaces)

Here's our first encounter with a "nested if" – that is, an "if" inside another "if". When we run this program, Python checks on line 4 whether the "a" variable contains the number 2. All of the code underneath it is indented, as a code block, to make it clear that it all belongs to the "if" statement on line 4.

But look at what happens on line 6: we then introduce another "if" statement, which compares the "name" variable with the string "Bob". If that condition is true, we open a new code block that belongs to line 6's "if", with another level of indentation – eight spaces instead of four. Then we print the message on line 7.

So look again at the indentation here: line 6's "if" is already part of the code block that starts with line 4's "if". So if "a" doesn't contain 2, Python won't even look at the following lines of indented code, and as there's nothing after that code, Python will end the program. If "a" does contain 2, however, then the "if" comparison on line 6 will be executed – and if that matches as well, both "print" instructions in the program will be executed. Here's a flowchart to clarify exactly what happens:

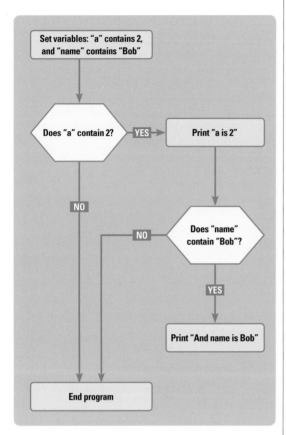

When we run Listing 18, the "a is bigger than..." message is only displayed if we enter a number bigger than 5.

More, less, equal to, or not?

We've looked at the "==" comparison operator to check if two things are the same, but there are a few other options as well. For instance, with numbers you may not want to check if a variable contains a number, but whether it's larger or smaller than it. Listing 18 uses a ">" symbol to check if a variable is greater than a specific number:

LISTING 18:

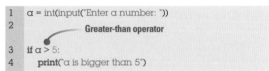

```
1   a = int(input("Enter a number: "))
2                       Greater-than operator
3   if a > 5:
4       print("a is bigger than 5")
```

Here we ask the user to input something, convert the string into a number, and then perform a comparison on line 3. In this case, we're saying: if the content of the "a" variable is greater than 5, execute the following indented code block. If "a" is equal to or smaller than 5, skip the indented code block (and the program ends).

Listing 19 shows some other comparisons you can perform in your code, with the specific meaning explained in the comments to the right.

LISTING 19:

```
1   if a < 5: # less than
2   if a >= 5: # greater than or equal to
3   if a <= 5: # less than or equal to
```

So if you perform the comparison on line 2 here, and "a" contains 5 or any greater value, then the code you add in the indented block underneath will be executed.

Sometimes you may not be interested in whether a comparison matches, or is greater than or less than – you just want to know if something is not equal. In Python we use the "!=" (exclamation mark equals) operator for this, like so:

LISTING 20:

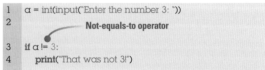

```
1   a = int(input("Enter the number 3: "))
2                       Not-equals-to operator
3   if a != 3:
4       print("That was not 3!")
```

Here we ask the user to input a number and convert it to an integer as usual. We then do a test: if the user has typed anything other than 3, we print a message. But if the user did enter 3, then line 4 (and any other following indented code) will not be executed.

CHANGING THE FLOW
More conditional statements

Back in Listing 17, we nested one "if" statement inside another to check whether two conditions are true. But imagine you want to check for more conditions – maybe three or four things, or even more. If you keep nesting them inside each other, you will need a lot of indentation and the code can start to look a bit weird.

Fortunately, there's a more elegant way to do this, using "and" and "or" operators in your conditional statements. For instance, here's a variant of Listing 17 where we use a strategically placed "and" to join two comparisons together:

LISTING 21:

```
1   a = 2
2   name = "Bob"
3                        Combines two "if" operations into one

4   if a == 2 and name == "Bob":
5       print("a is 2")
6       print("And name is Bob")
```

In this example, we do both of our comparisons together on line 4: only if "a" contains 2 and "name" contains "Bob" does Python then execute the indented code beneath. And because it's all done in a single "if" operation, we don't need to perform separate checks with multiple levels of indentation. That's a lot tidier, isn't it?

Now, "and" here has a counterpart and its name is "or". Have a look at Listing 22 and see if you can guess what happens:

LISTING 22:

```
1   a = 9000
2   name = "Bob"
3                        This "if" succeeds if one (or both) of
                         the comparisons is true

4   if a == 2 or name == "Bob":
5       print("a is 2")
6       print("Or name is Bob")
```

We've set "a" to contain 9000 in this case, so it certainly won't match the "a == 2" comparison in line 4. However,

in line 4 we've used "or" this time – so Python only cares if one of the comparisons happens to be true. Because "name" contains "Bob", one of the two comparisons is correct, and therefore the indented code block underneath gets executed.

Alternatives to if: elif and else

Another way to combine multiple "if" operations is to use "elif", which is short for "else if". It basically means: if the first "if" operation didn't succeed, let's try another "if". As an example, let's say we have a program that processes scores in a sports tournament, and gives out grades accordingly. If a player gets 50 or more points, he/she gets an A grade. 40–49 points is a B grade, and anything below that is a C.

It's possible to do this with a series of "if" statements as we've explored previously, either nesting them or using various "and" and "or" operators. But using "if" combined

Chaining and organizing comparisons

In Listings 21 and 22, we've performed two comparisons together, but you can add as many "and" and "or" operators as you like. Indeed, you can build up rather powerful comparison operations by using brackets to lump some comparisons together. For instance:

```
if (a == 1 and b == 2) or (x == 3 and y == 4):
```

Here, we're bundling the "a" and "b" comparisons into a single one, and the "x" and "y" comparisons into another. So Python shortens this down to two operations: whether "a" and "b" contain 1 and 2, or whether "x" and "y" are 3 and 4.

So if you change "a" and "b" to something else, but leave "x" and "y" as 3 and 4, the comparison will still be true. Conversely, if you leave "a" and "b" containing 1 and 2, but change "x" and "y", the comparison will also be true.

with "elif" leads to a really clean and understandable program, like in Listing 23:

LISTING 23:

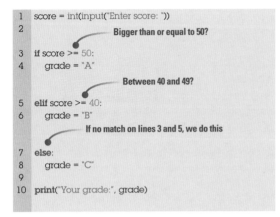

```
1    score = int(input("Enter score: "))
2                          Bigger than or equal to 50?

3    if score >= 50:
4        grade = "A"
                          Between 40 and 49?

5    elif score >= 40:
6        grade = "B"
                          If no match on lines 3 and 5, we do this

7    else:
8        grade = "C"
9
10   print("Your grade:", grade)
```

After getting a score from the user, the first thing this program does, on line 3, is check to see whether the score is equal to or greater than 50. If this is the case, we assign the letter "A" to a new "grade" variable, and the entire "if" operation finishes. Python doesn't pay attention to any other "elif" or "else" operations in this chunk of code – it simply skips down to the next non-"if"-related code, which is on line 10.

However, if the score is not equal to or greater than 50 on line 3, we present Python with another "if" on line 5, as

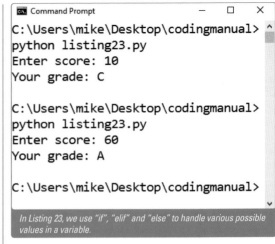

an alternative. This "elif" instruction says: OK, the previous "if" comparison on line 3 didn't work, so we know that the score isn't 50 or above. But is it at least 40? If so, assign the letter "B" to the "grade" variable, and skip the "else" section below – jump ahead to line 10.

Now, if the "elif" on line 5 doesn't match either, we provide a default grade in line 7, using "else". When put at the end of "if" and "elif" operations, this "else" simply means: perform the following indented code if none of the previous conditions matched. So this "else" code will only be executed if the score is less than 40. This flowchart clarifies exactly what happens:

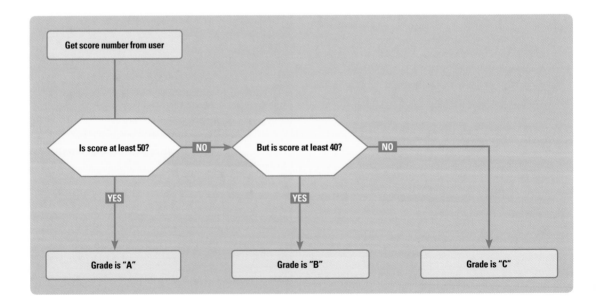

Note that the "elif" on line 5 only gets executed by the Python interpreter if the previous "if" on line 3 doesn't match. But what happens if we use a plain "if" on line 5 instead of "elif"? Well, it would always be executed – regardless of what happens before, because it starts a new "if" block. So if the score was 80, then both "if" operations on lines 3 and 5 would match, and the grade would end up being "B" as that's the most recent "if" statement. But by using "elif" instead, we make sure that the minimum of 50 for "A" has already been tested for, so by line 5's "elif" we know the score is definitely 49 or smaller.

Case-insensitive text comparisons

Earlier in this section we performed a few comparisons of text strings – such as in line 6 of Listing 17. But one thing we didn't check for is the case, i.e. whether or not upper- or lower-case characters have been entered. If we change line 2 so that "Bob" becomes "bob" (all lower case), then it won't match the comparison on line 6, and line 7 won't be executed. Python is very picky about case in situations like this, so we have to be careful.

However, there's a solution. During the "if" comparison, we can use a lower-case version of the "name" variable and compare that with the lower-case "bob" string, like so:

```
if name.lower() == "bob":
```

This ".lower()" bit that we add on to the "name" variable is called a method, and we'll explore methods later in the book. But for now, just be aware that it **temporarily** generates a lower-case string based on the contents of "name" for comparison (without changing the contents of the variable permanently).

So whether the user entered "Bob", "BOB" or "Bob", for the sake of this "if" comparison the user has entered "bob". This gives us something easy to check against – an all-lower-case string – so that we don't have to perform separate checks for every combination of "Bob", "bOb" etc.

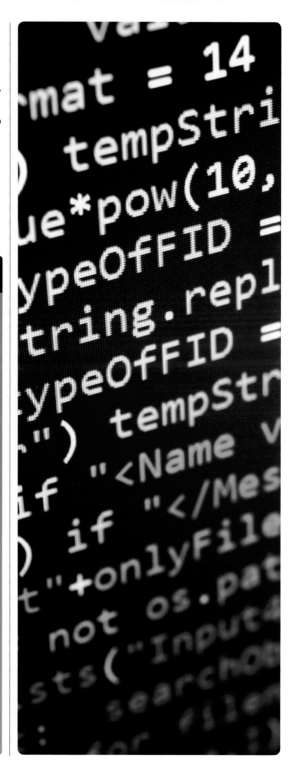

CHANGING THE FLOW
Repetition with loops

One thing computers do especially well is repeating a sequence of instructions. Again and again and again. It's not just about speed – although processors do many calculations orders of magnitude faster than our grey matter can – but the main benefit is that computers can't get bored. No matter how trivial the job is, and no matter how many times you tell the computer to repeat it, the job gets done. The computer doesn't lose interest and decide to tackle a different task (well, not at the moment – let's see how artificial intelligence develops over the next few years...).

If we want to repeat an instruction in Python, or indeed a big bunch of instructions, there are various commands and tools at our disposal. Some of these simply repeat the instructions until a certain condition is met; others perform more intricate operations, changing variables with each iteration of the process. Every time a bunch of instructions is repeated, we call this a "loop" – you'll see exactly why we use this term in a moment...

The "while" loop

One of the simplest ways to repeat a set of instructions is to use a "while" instruction, followed by an indented code block. For instance, let's say we want to display the numbers 1 to 10 on the screen. We could do this using 10 separate "print" instructions – but that would be rather wasteful. Thanks to "while", we can do the job in a smaller chunk of code, as you can see in Listing 24:

LISTING 24:

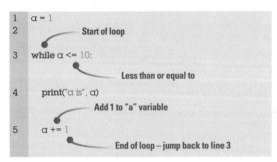

In this code, we create a variable called "a" and set its value to 1. Then, on line 3, we start a new loop. This line of code says: while the contents of "a" are less than or equal to 10, execute the following (indented) code block. So when this program starts, "a" is only 1, so it's certainly less

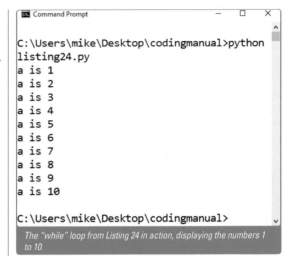

The "while" loop from Listing 24 in action, displaying the numbers 1 to 10.

than or equal to 10! Consequently, we print the contents of "a" to the screen in line 4, and then add 1 to "a" in line 5.

But what happens at the end of this indented code block? Well, Python jumps (or "loops") back to line 3, to perform the check again. This time "a" contains 2, but it's still way less than 10 so Python executes the code block once more, and loops back to the top. Indeed, it keeps doing this until "a" is 11, at which point the condition in the "while" instruction on line 3 doesn't match, so the code block doesn't get executed. And as there's nothing after the code block, that's the end of the program. So we have the numbers 1 to 10 on the screen as intended.

Here's a flowchart depicting exactly what happens:

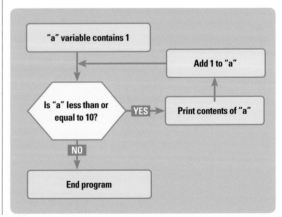

Tip

When starting a "while" loop you can use many other comparisons, such as those in Listings 19 and 20. For instance, we could change Listing 24's "while" line from 'while "a" is less than or equal to 10' to an alternative: 'while "a" is not 11'. For this we would put "while a != 11" on line 3, and the program will still output the same results, terminating the loop as soon as "a" contains 11.

Checks and loops within loops

It's possible to put multiple "while" loops inside each other, or add "if" checks, or indeed any other Python code. Let's modify Listing 24 so that we only display even numbers. What's the best way to do that? One solution is to use the modulo operation to perform a division and get a remainder. If we divide "a" by 2, and there's no remainder, then clearly "a" contains an even number. So our new code is in Listing 25:

LISTING 25:

```
1    a = 1
2
3    while a <= 10:
                    Check if remainder of "a" divided by 2 is zero
4        if a % 2 == 0:
5            print("a is", a)
6
7        a += 1
```

Line 4 does all the magic here: we divide the current contents of the "a" variable by 2, and if there's no remainder (i.e. it's zero) then we know "a" is an even number. This program prints 2, 4, 6, 8 and 10 to the screen.

Tip

In Listing 25, we've left line 6 blank for readability, to show that line 7 has nothing to do with the "if" code beforehand. But because line 7 is still indented with four spaces, Python knows that it's definitely part of the overall "while" loop.

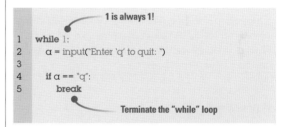

```
Command Prompt                           —    □    ×

C:\Users\mike\Desktop\codingmanual>python
listing26.py
Enter 'q' to quit: a
Enter 'q' to quit: c
Enter 'q' to quit: help!
Enter 'q' to quit: 1234567
Enter 'q' to quit: Hmm...
Enter 'q' to quit: q

C:\Users\mike\Desktop\codingmanual>
```

Using the "break" command, we can exit an infinite loop when a certain condition is matched.

Infinite loops and breaking out

Sometimes you may want to create a loop that carries on being executed forever, until you explicitly tell it to stop. We can use "while" for this, giving it a condition that is always true. And to break out of the "while" loop, we can use the aptly named "break" instruction, like in Listing 26:

LISTING 26:

```
                              1 is always 1!
1    while 1:
2        a = input("Enter 'q' to quit: ")
3
4        if a == "q":
5            break
                              Terminate the "while" loop
```

Try running this program – it will keep prompting you to enter a letter, and only stop when you enter "q". But what's going on with the odd "while 1" in line 1? Imagine it as "while 1 == 1" – so because 1 is always 1, regardless of what happens in the program, the loop is always executed (an "infinite loop"). The only thing that can stop it is a "break" command, as we use in line 5.

For loops

Another type of loop is called "for". It works with a series of numbers or text strings. For each number or string, "for" executes the loop and when there are no more numbers or strings left, the loop ends. To make this work, we need to create a special type of variable that contains a Python "list" – a collection of pieces of data – like in Listing 27:

LISTING 27:

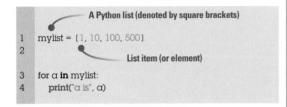

```
     A Python list (denoted by square brackets)
1   mylist = [1, 10, 100, 500]
2
            List item (or element)
3   for a in mylist:
4       print("a is", a)
```

We cover lists in more detail later, but here's a quick overview of using them in "for" loops. Here we create a new list containing four items (or "elements" as they are sometimes known): the numbers 1, 10, 100 and 500. To tell Python that these items belong to a list, we put square brackets around them, and separate them with commas.

Next, in line 3, we set up a new "for" loop. This creates a new variable called "a", and Python executes the loop for each item in the list, copying the item into "a" each time. So in the first iteration of the loop, "a" contains 1. In the next, "a" contains 10, in the next 100, and in the final iteration 500. You can change the contents of "mylist" on line 1 to add or remove numbers, which will then change how many times the loop is executed.

So as you can see, "for" loops offer more versatility than "while" loops: instead of just doing things a set number of times, you can work with specific numbers. This is especially useful if you have multiple lists that correspond to each other, like in a spreadsheet: you might have a list of 100 names (lists can contain text strings too) and a list of 100 scores. You can then go through the lists to generate grades accordingly.

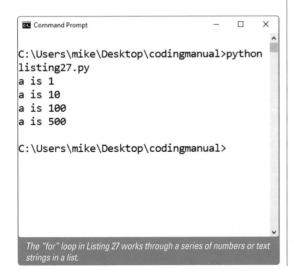

The "for" loop in Listing 27 works through a series of numbers or text strings in a list.

Another loop option: ranges

You've seen that "for" loops can work with existing lists of data. But what about cases where you don't have any data to hand, but you want to perform a loop based on a series of numbers anyway? This is where Python's "range" function comes in mightily handy. Essentially, "range" lets you create a list of numbers on the fly – so you can use the list directly in a "for" loop. Consider Listing 28, where we do just that:

LISTING 28:

```
1   for a in range(1, 11):
2       print("a is", a)
```

This performs exactly the same job as in Listing 24 – displaying the numbers 1 to 10 on the screen – but in a shorter and more elegant fashion. With the "range" function, we provide two parameters: the starting number, and the number when the loop should end plus 1. For each iteration of this loop, our "a" variable gets a new value, starting with 1 and ending with 10. As soon as "a" contains 11, the loop ends.

When you use two parameters with "range", the content of the variable is incremented each loop – so "a" goes up by 1 during each loop in our case. However, if you specify a third parameter, this is used to define the **size** of the increment each loop (how much should be added on each time). What do you think Listing 29 does?

LISTING 29:

```
1   for a in range(1, 11, 3):
2       print("a is", a)
3
4   for b in range(10, 0, -1):
5       print("b is", b)
```

In the first "for" loop, we tell Python to add 3 to the "a" variable after each loop – so it displays the numbers 1, 4, 7 and 10. In the second "for" loop, we start the "range" with 10 and end with zero, using a -1 (minus one) change to the "b" variable each time. So this displays the numbers 10 to 1 in descending order. It might look a bit odd at first, but try experimenting with different numbers and see what results you get.

 CHALLENGE YOURSELF

1. To compare a variable with a number, which is correct: "if a == 2" or "if a = 2"?

2. Should you use tabs or spaces for indentation in Python?

3. What does "if a <= 5" mean?

4. What do you append to a string variable name, to perform a lower-case comparison?

5. What instruction can you use to escape an infinite loop?

04.

Save time with functions

In this section

Creating simple functions   **44**
Multiple functions and loops

. . . .

Passing parameters   **47**
Variables and multiple parameters
Getting data back

. . . .

Variable scope   **50**
Local vs global

. . . .

Fun with built-in functions   **51**
exec – run a program within a program
chr – display fancy characters
len – get the length of a string
pow and round – extra math functions

. . . .

Challenge yourself   **53**

. . . .

As we dive into section 4, your Python skills are starting to get well fleshed-out. You're now able to write programs that can process different types of data – whether built in to the program or supplied from the user via "input" – and then act on the data accordingly using "if" operations. In addition, you can repeat operations in various ways with loops. So far so good, but now it's time to explore another fundamental of programming, and one that applies to most major languages: functions.

Modularity in programming is essential when you start working on larger projects, and functions help you to achieve this modularity. In this way, instead of your program being a giant list of instructions with the odd "if", "while" and "for" in there to change the flow, you can break up your program's functionality into separate pieces which can operate semi-independently. For instance, if you're working on a program to handle registrations for an event, you may want to separate out the bits of code that handle screen display, the bits that read and write data to your drive, and so forth.

By dividing up these tasks into individual, mostly self-contained, code chunks called functions, you can work on them separately, encourage others to work on them (without needing to know how the rest of the program works), and even reuse functions you create in your other programs. This is what modularity is all about – and it's a real time-saver in coding. We've already used some of Python's built-in functions like "print" and "input", so let's look at creating new ones from scratch.

SAVE TIME WITH FUNCTIONS
Creating simple functions

The best way to understand how functions work is to see one in action. In your text editor, enter the code in Listing 30 into "test.py" as usual and then run it:

LISTING 30:

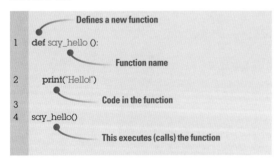

```
1   def say_hello ():
2       print("Hello!")
3
4   say_hello()
```

Defines a new function

Function name

Code in the function

This executes (calls) the function

In order to create a function that we can use in our program, we first need to define it – hence the "def" at the start of line 1. This tells Python: let's create a new function, and give it a name, in this case "say_hello". We also then put open and close brackets after the name, for reasons we'll come to in a moment. And finally, we end the line with a colon (:), which indicates the start of an indented

block of code, just like in the "if" operations and "while" loops we saw earlier.

And then the function's code begins! In our case, we just display a simple message on the screen. As with all code blocks, indentation is critical here: the function's code must have at least one level of indentation (i.e. four spaces) to distinguish it from the rest of the code. Of course, if you then decide to add "if" operations and loops in the function, you will need to add further levels of indentation accordingly. Our "say_hello" function clearly ends on line 2, because the code after it is not indented.

Now, it's very important to note here that the function isn't automatically executed by Python when we run this program. All we've done on lines 1 and 2 is define it – i.e. make Python aware of its existence. As far as Python is concerned, we have defined this function for our own use later on, but we may not even use it at all. If this particular program ended on line 2, and you ran it, nothing would happen.

So on line 4, we execute – or "call" – our function, to make Python process it. We simply place the name of the function along with the brackets. When Python reads line 4, it thinks: OK, time to execute "say_hello" that was

In Listing 30, we move "print" out of the main body of code, and into a separate function.

defined earlier. Once "say_hello" has finished on line 2, Python jumps back to the main code, starting on line 5, but because that doesn't exist in our code, the program simply terminates.

Multiple functions and loops

You can define as many functions as you want (well, until your computer runs out of memory!), and call them as many times as you want to. In Listing 31, we create two functions, add a loop to the second one to demonstrate multiple levels of indentation, and then have three function calls:

LISTING 31:

```
        First function
1   def say_hello():
2       print("Hello!")
        Second function
3
4   def count_to_10():
5       for a in range(1, 11):
6           print(a)
7
8   say_hello()
9   count_to_10()
10  say_hello()
```

You know what the code inside these two functions does from the previous sections of this book, so let's go straight to line 8, the first non-function line – as this is where Python starts running the program. We first call "say_hello", then "count_to_10" and then "say_hello" again. So we end

> **ⓘ Tip**
>
> What names can you give to functions? The rules are very much the same as for variables: they can't start with a number, can't include punctuation and shouldn't have the same name as an existing Python keyword or function. (So if you try to define your own function called "print", expect a lot of problems!) It's also a good idea to have descriptive function names with words separated by underscores. So a function that gets the user's name could be called "get_users_name", for instance.

up with "Hello!" on the screen, followed by the numbers 1 to 10, and then "Hello!" once more.

You may be thinking at this point: why do the functions have to go at the top, when they're not executed straight away? Why not have the main code at the top, and then the functions later on? Well, think of it from the perspective of the Python interpreter: if you put the main code at the top, so that the program starts with a call to "say_hello", Python has never seen that function before. Where is it? Is it a built-in Python function? Is it somewhere else in this code file, or perhaps another file?

But by placing the function definitions at the top of the file, Python becomes aware of them straight away, and remembers where they are for later usage. When you call a function in your main code, Python knows immediately where to find that function – without having to do a search.

```
Command Prompt                    —    □    ×
C:\Users\mike\Desktop\codingmanual>python
listing31.py
Hello!
1
2
3
4
5
6
7
8
9
10
Hello!

C:\Users\mike\Desktop\codingmanual>
```
We can define multiple functions, and call them arbitrarily – as seen in Listing 31.

When a function calls another

It's not only possible for one function to call another but it's very much encouraged for the modular program design that we described at the start of this section. Of course, when you have one function calling another one, which in turn may call yet another function, you have to keep a close eye on the program flow. You can often end up far away from your main code – which can make identifying and fixing problems tricky!

Anyway, let's see this in action. Change lines 1 and 2 in Listing 31 to this:

```
def say_hello():
    count_to_10()
```

Now run Listing 31 again, and you can see that the lists of numbers 1 to 10 appear three times on the screen. Our "say_hello" function does nothing other than call "count_to_10" – redirecting execution of the code to another function. Note that when "count_to_10" finishes, it hands control back to the piece of code that called it. So when "count_to_10" is called from inside "say_hello", when the former finishes, execution jumps back to the latter. And because we

don't do anything else inside "say_hello", execution then jumps back to the main code (line 9).

One thing you also need to be aware of is infinite recursion. If you call the same function inside itself, Python will not be happy:

```
def say_hello():
    say_hello()
```

In this case, Python will try to execute "say_hello" a certain number of times before giving up angrily with an error like "RecursionError: maximum recursion depth exceeded". Why does this happen? It's to do with memory: each time your program calls "say_hello", Python needs to remember where to go back to when the function has finished.

Because we keep calling the same function inside itself, every time it runs it needs to remember a new bit of information, and your computer will eventually run out of memory! Hence Python complains instead. (Note that in some rare cases it's useful to call a function inside of itself, but only for very advanced code – we won't need to do that.)

SAVE TIME WITH FUNCTIONS
Passing parameters

So far, our functions have been pretty basic: they just do one thing, and the same thing, no matter how and when they're called. This is fine for many functions, but wouldn't it be more useful if you could influence what they do? Wouldn't it be great if you could send (or "pass") bits of data to them, so that they can process the data and act accordingly? Thanks to parameters, and the parentheses (brackets) we used earlier in the function definition, this is totally possible.

In Listing 32 we have our first example of a function that receives some data from the calling code, in the form of a parameter:

LISTING 32:

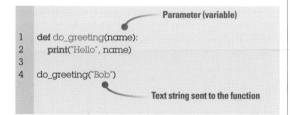

Parameter (variable)

```
1  def do_greeting(name):
2      print("Hello", name)
3
4  do_greeting("Bob")
```

Text string sent to the function

Here we define a function called "do_greeting" that takes one parameter – i.e. one piece of data from the code that calls the function. Because we don't know exactly what will be sent from the calling code, we create a new variable here called "name" and put it inside the brackets. This basically tells Python: whenever the main code calls this

"do_greeting" function, put whatever is sent to it inside the "name" variable.

Then, on line 2, we simply print a greeting along with the contents of the variable, as we saw earlier in the book. Now look at line 4: here's where we call our "do_greeting" function, but instead of just having brackets with nothing inside like in the previous listings, this time we place a text string that we send to the function.

So when Python processes this program, its thought process is like so: "OK, there's a function called 'do_greeting', which takes one piece of data that I should put into the 'name' variable, before printing it. But where does the program actually start? Ah, on line 4, the first bit of code outside of a function. The program wants me to run the 'do_greeting' function, and send the text 'Bob' to it. So I'll run 'do_greeting', and put 'Bob' inside the 'name' variable."

Variables and multiple parameters
As well as sending direct data, like the "Bob" text string in Listing 32, we can also send the contents of a variable. Listing 33 shows an example of this:

LISTING 33:

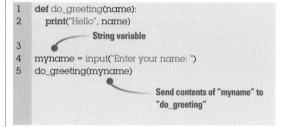

```
1  def do_greeting(name):
2      print("Hello", name)
3
4  myname = input("Enter your name: ")
5  do_greeting(myname)
```

String variable

Send contents of "myname" to "do_greeting"

In this case, we use Python's built-in "input" function to get the user's name into a variable called "myname". On line 5, we send the contents of that variable to the "do_greeting" function. So whatever the user types in line 4 will end up being stored in the "name" variable in "do_greeting".

Functions become especially powerful when they process multiple pieces of data. So far our functions have just had one parameter – one variable inside the brackets in the definition – but we can add many more. Have a look at Listing 34, which uses a function that takes two bits of data instead of one:

Tip

We encourage you to experiment with and make changes to all code listings in this book, to see what happens, but a quick note! When you're playing with the code in Listing 32, you may be tempted to use the contents of the "name" variable from "do_greeting" outside of the function here, e.g. after line 4. But you'll receive an error message. This is because "name" is only accessible inside the function – we'll explain this later on.

LISTING 34:

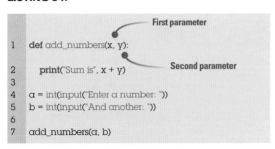

```
1   def add_numbers(x, y):

2     print("Sum is", x + y)
3
4   a = int(input("Enter a number: "))
5   b = int(input("And another: "))
6
7   add_numbers(a, b)
```

First parameter · Second parameter

```
Command Prompt                        —    □    ×

C:\Users\mike\Desktop\codingmanual>python
listing34.py
Enter a number: 1
And another: 5
Sum is 6

C:\Users\mike\Desktop\codingmanual>python
listing34.py
Enter a number: 50
And another: 200
Sum is 250

C:\Users\mike\Desktop\codingmanual>
```

It's possible to send multiple pieces of data to a function, as demonstrated in Listing 34, where we pass two integer numbers.

Our function definition on line 1 here tells Python that "add_numbers" should expect two bits of information to be sent to it, which it should store in new "x" and "y" variables. This function does a trivial job – just adding the numbers together and printing the result – but it demonstrates how the multiple parameters are received and processed.

So on lines 4 and 5 we get two numbers from the user and store them in variables "a" and "b", and then on line 7, we call our previously defined "add_numbers" function using the contents of "a" and "b". When Python runs "add_numbers", the contents of "a" are placed into "x", and the contents of "b" are placed into "y".

 A backup plan: default parameters

Here's a useful trick. When you define a new function, and you specify the data it receives into a variable, you can set default values for that data if the calling program doesn't specify it explicitly. The best way to understand this is to look at Listing 35:

LISTING 35:

```
1   def do_greeting(name = "Unknown user"):

2     print("Hello", name)
3
4   do_greeting("Bob")
5   do_greeting()
```

This is very much like Listing 32 we saw earlier, but we've elaborated on the "name" variable in the parameter section of the function definition. Here we're telling Python: place whatever's sent to "do_greeting" in the "name" variable, but if nothing is sent, put the string "Unknown user" inside the "name" variable instead.

So when the main code execution begins with line 4, our "do_greeting" function spits out "Hello Bob"

as planned. On line 5, however, we don't explicitly provide a text string to "do_greeting"; we just have nothing inside the brackets. So when Python runs "do_greeting" this time, the function spots that the calling code has given no parameters, and puts "Unknown user" into the "name" variable instead.

But what is this useful for? There are a couple of benefits: if you're writing a function that will mostly deal with the default values, and only rarely need custom data sent to it, you can set up a function like this and the calling code will be shorter and tidier. (As in, most calls to the function won't need lots of parameters.) Note that you can specify default values for multiple parameters – whether they're text strings or numbers.

Alternatively, default values can be useful when you're debugging a large program. They can allow a function to run (or at least try to run!) even if the calling program has forgotten to provide data. This is especially useful when multiple people are working on a program, and one coder is calling a function written by another coder who may have forgotten exactly which parameters to pass.

Getting data back

Up until this point, our programs have only sent data to functions and have not expected anything in return. This makes sense if you just want to display something on the screen as in our code listings, but what if you want the function to do some processing and hand information back to the main program, without displaying anything? The technique for this is called "returning" data – that is, when a function sends back a "return value".

For example, in Listing 34 our "add_numbers" function took two parameters (number variables), added them together, and displayed the results on the screen. Let's now tweak it so that it doesn't print anything itself, but instead sends the results back to the calling code in the main program.

LISTING 36:

```
1    def add_numbers(x, y):
2        z = x + y
                    Send contents of "z" back to calling code

3        return z
4
5    a = int(input("Enter a number: "))
6    b = int(input("And another: "))
7
                Store number sent back into this "c" variable

8    c = add_numbers(a, b)
9    print("Sum is:", c)
```

Here we've modified our "add_numbers" function and introduced a new variable: "z". We place the sum of "x" and "y" – the two numbers that are sent to the function – into this "z" variable. Then we perform the magic on line 3: we tell Python to send the contents of "z" back to the part of the code that called this function. This is the aforementioned "return value" – hence the instruction "return".

But how do we store the data that's sent back from the function? Look at line 8: this time we not only call our "add_numbers" function with the two parameters it needs but, with the equals (=) sign, we also assign the result to a new "c" variable. So Python processes line 8 from right to left: it runs "add_numbers", and when that function has finished and sent back a number with the "return" instruction, Python places that number into "c".

Functions can return numerical values as we've seen in Listing 36, but you can also use text as well – the choice is all up to you and depends entirely on the needs of your program. Indeed, it's also possible for a function to send

Tip

The technique we use on line 8 of Listing 36 isn't actually completely new to us – we first came across it back in Listing 11, when we got input from a user. The equals (=) sign is doing the same job in both cases; in Listing 11, we're simply getting the text string return value from Python's built-in "input" function. So whether we're getting data back from our own functions or those included in Python, the technique is the same.

back multiple bits of data (e.g. several numbers or strings of text), but we'll explore that later when we deal with Python's advanced data types.

Anyway, now you can start to really appreciate the power and flexibility of functions. You're learning the essential building blocks of programming here, and when you start to write longer programs, you can create functions to perform specific tasks. As an example, you might be working on some code that regularly needs to perform a set of complex mathematical operations. By putting it all into a function, you can call it whenever you need it but keep it separate from the main code. And even better, you could use that function in a different programming project one day.

Listing 36 is a lot like Listing 34, but this time our function sends back a "return value" -for the main code to print.

SAVE TIME WITH FUNCTIONS
Variable scope

Earlier on we talked about the importance of modularity, where pieces of code (such as functions) are isolated from one another, can be moved around and changed without affecting the rest of the program, and can be copied into other programs as we just mentioned. But to really make a function modular, it needs to be sure that it doesn't accidentally overwrite data elsewhere.

Look back at Listing 36 for a moment: we use different variables in the "add_number" function and the main code for clarity. What happens if we try to reuse variables? Have a guess at what happens when you run Listing 37:

LISTING 37:

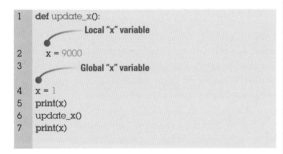

```
1   def update_x():
                     Local "x" variable

2       x = 9000
3                Global "x" variable

4   x = 1
5   print(x)
6   update_x()
7   print(x)
```

This program seems straightforward enough: when execution begins on line 4, we create a new "x" variable and set its value to 1. We then print the contents of "x", and then call our "update_x" function which sets "x" to 9000. When that function completes, execution continues on line 7, which prints... "1". What on earth is going on here? Why didn't "update_x" do its job properly?

 Tip

If you have a function that's executed hundreds or thousands of times, you may be wondering what happens to all the local copies of variables – do they just eat up memory forever? Fortunately, no. Whenever Python finishes executing a function, all of the local variables are "freed" in memory to make space. If you want to keep the value of a variable across multiple calls to a function, you will need to mark it as global as we discuss in a moment.

The crux is this: every time we call "update_x" and line 2 is executed, it creates its own "local" "x" variable, which is separate from the main code. Whatever "update_x" does with its own "x" has no effect on the "x" we created in the main code on line 4. And the reason for this is simple: it keeps the code modular.

Imagine a large program with lots of functions that use many different variables. If those functions weren't using their own versions of variables, they could accidentally overwrite variables used elsewhere in the program – especially when a program is using a lot of common variable names such as "a", "b", "filename" etc.

Local vs global

So by making this distinction, we can introduce functions into a program – possibly from another program – and be sure that they won't trample all over our data whenever they're called. If we have an "x" variable in our main code that's extremely important to us, and we call a function written by someone else that also happens to use a variable called "x", we know that our data won't be changed without us knowing. (Otherwise we'd have the most horrendously difficult debugging tasks ahead of us!) Listing 38 also demonstrates how variables work inside and outside of functions:

LISTING 38:

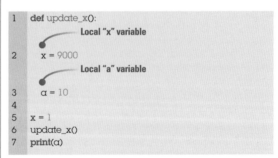

```
1   def update_x():
                     Local "x" variable

2       x = 9000
                     Local "a" variable

3       a = 10
4
5   x = 1
6   update_x()
7   print(a)
```

This is actually a broken program! You see, it runs until line 7, when we try to print the contents of the "a" variable. The problem is, there is no "a" variable in the main code – only inside the "update_x" function. But that variable is just specific to that function, so it's not available to us anywhere else.

This concept of where variables can be used is known

as "variable scope": a variable that's only available inside a single function is known as local (like the "a" variable here), whereas a variable that can be used (and updated) everywhere is known as global. Any variable you create outside of a function will be global by default – you don't need to specify it.

But there's one thing we haven't covered yet: what if we want to use a global variable inside a function, like with "x" on line 2 of Listing 37, and not just the function's own version of the variable? This requires a different approach. To tell Python that we want to actually use the global variable, we add the "global" keyword like so:

LISTING 39:

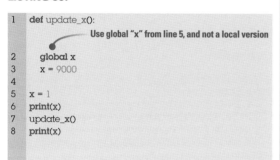

```
1    def update_x():
                    Use global "x" from line 5, and not a local version
2        global x
3        x = 9000
4
5    x = 1
6    print(x)
7    update_x()
8    print(x)
```

 Tip

You might be tempted to use global variables throughout your programs, to avoid having to remember which are global and which are local. Why not just chuck them all into the start of the main code, and let functions update them as they please? Sure, at the start of a project it may save time, when you only have a small number of variables to juggle. But as time goes on, you may find functions you wrote long ago having adverse effects on the rest of the code. And it'd be even harder to reuse those functions elsewhere. So the best coding practice is to only use global variables where absolutely necessary – try to keep things modular!

This is very much the same as in Listing 37, but with one crucial addition: the "global x" on line 2. This tells Python that the "x" variable in this function should be the global one created elsewhere, and not a local version. So when this program is run, line 6 first displays "x" as 1, and then our call to "update_x" updates the global "x" created on line 5. By the time line 8 is run, "x" contains 9000.

SAVE TIME WITH FUNCTIONS
Fun with built-in functions

Let's now take a break from looking at the workings of Python, and turn our attention to some of the other built-in functions that the language provides. Using these we can already start to create some quite powerful programs – and it's fun to just play around with them as well. We've already used a few built-in functions such as "print" and "input", but there are others that are also worth exploring. Let's see what they do.

exec – run a program within a program
Using the "exec" function, you can tell Python to interpret and execute the code inside a text string on the fly. This might sound a bit odd at first, so take a look at Listing 40 which demonstrates it in action:

LISTING 40:

```
                    Create blank string variable
1    code = ""
2    x = 1
3
4    while code != "exit":
5        code = input("Enter some code: ")
                    Execute whatever's in the variable
6        exec(code)
7        x += 1
```

In the first line, we create a new string variable called "code" that's completely empty – hence the two quote (")

A Python program running Python code inside of itself! Listing 40 shows how this is done, using the built-in "exec" function.

marks. We need to create this in advance, because when we start a loop on line 4, we check the contents of this variable. Had we not created "code" earlier, Python would be confused and not sure where it came from.

Next, on line 5 we get input from the user and store it in the "code" variable. Then line 6 performs the magic: it tells Python to execute the contents of "code" just like any other Python code. So whatever you type at the prompt will be executed – try entering "print" instructions, for instance. Note that "exec" doesn't run the code as an entirely separate program, but as part of the current one – so if you enter "print(x)" at the input prompt, it will show the value of "x" which is incremented with each loop, to demonstrate how this works. In more practical terms, you could use a snippet of code like this for interactive debugging and checking variables during program execution. (Enter "exit" to stop the program.)

chr – display fancy characters

If your program just needs to display common characters like the letters A–Z, numbers, punctuation marks and so forth, you'll be fine with your keyboard and normal "print" calls. But what about lesser-used characters or symbols, especially those from foreign languages? Or characters that have become more common in recent years, but aren't necessarily on every keyboard?

The euro sign (€) is a good example of this. If you need to output it in your program, but don't have it on your keyboard, you may be stumped. Go to the Wikipedia page for it at **https://en.wikipedia.org/wiki/Euro_sign**, however, and you'll see that it's available in HTML as

"€". The number here is Unicode, a standard for encoding and representing text, and we can use that number in Python via the "chr" function like so:

LISTING 41:

```
1  print(chr(8364))
```

Note: if you're using the Windows Command Prompt, you'll need to enter "cmd /K chcp 65001" beforehand to make this work (it changes the character set that's available).

Et voila, the "€" symbol appears on the screen. You can discover more Unicode characters at **https://en.wikipedia.org/wiki/List_of_Unicode_characters** – but that page is a little dull, so let's have some fun! Let's display a lot of Unicode characters:

LISTING 42:

```
1  for x in range(32, 1000):
2      print(chr(x), end="")
```

This program prints every Unicode character from 32 up to 1000 (earlier ones are non-printing). Note the extra parameter in the "print" function, which stops "print" from jumping to a new line after each character – you may find that useful in your own programs. Many of these Unicode characters are from various languages and will produce interesting output on your screen, like in the screenshot. Indeed, if your command prompt is a bit messed up after this, due to it being confused by all the characters, just close it and open a new one.

When you run Listing 42, you'll see a lot of gobbledygook on the screen – these are Unicode characters for various languages.

len – get the length of a string

We've been working with string variables, primarily with the "input" function. Often it's useful to get the length of those strings – i.e. how many individual characters are in them. Let's say you absolutely need to get a user's name, which means they have to type something and not just hit Enter at the "input" prompt for an empty string. You could force them to enter something like so, using the "len" function:

LISTING 43:

```
1   length = 0
2
3   while length == 0:
4       name = input("Enter your name: ")
                                Returns the length of the specified
                                string variable
5       length = len(name)
6
7   print("Hello", name)
```

In line 3 we set up a loop that runs as long as the "length" variable we created at the start contains zero. After each "input", we get the length of the inputted string using "len" on line 5. If the user tapped Enter at the "input" prompt, there are no characters in the string – so the length is zero and the loop continues. But if the user types something like "Bob", that is a string of three letters, so "length" no longer contains zero and the loop stops. Then we print the name.

pow and round – extra math functions

Finally, let's wrap up this section by working with some really big numbers. Python has a function called "pow" which takes two parameters, and returns the first number raised to the power of the second. Let's see it in action:

LISTING 44:

```
1   a = int(input("Enter a number: "))
2   b = int(input("And another: "))
3
            Return first number to
            power of second
4   print(a, "to the power of", b, "is", pow(a, b))
```

Here we get two integer numbers from the user, and then start a rather complex "print" function on line 4. We display the two variables and some text, and then display the results of "pow(a, b)" – i.e. we display what is returned from that function. By placing the "pow" function inside a call to the "print" function like this, we can use the result from "pow" directly, without storing it in a temporary variable.

So try entering numbers: 10 to the power of 2 is 100 (10 times 10), to the power of 3 is 1000 (10 times 10 times 10) and so on. Then try some big numbers – 1000 to the power of 1000, and you'll see that Python handles the results with ease. You can go even bigger, but at some point the Python interpreter might break out in a sweat and give up.

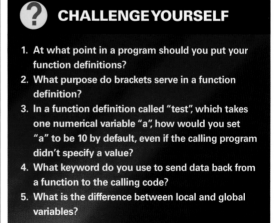

```
Command Prompt                              –  □  ×

C:\Users\mike\Desktop\codingmanual>python
listing44.py
Enter a number: 234
And another: 123
234 to the power of 123 is 259149551433081
14635177098802178395597060844178058237280 5
25326180902871561617613798668079351338163 9
18409967279895549091924890333446149846242 1
01414362105162172327462507242503789534024 6
00576103971859512134938220645562373823638 2
81210359896611908026405889059881413810140 8
5430056382104175172911104

C:\Users\mike\Desktop\codingmanual>
```

The "pow" function used in Listing 44 can generate some whoppingly big numbers.

Then there's "round", which we can use with floating-point numbers to round down the number of decimal places. Try running this program:

LISTING 45:

```
1   a = float(input("Enter a number: "))
                                Round down to three decimal places
2   print(round(a, 3))
```

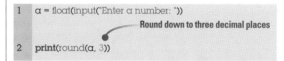

At the prompt, enter a number with lots of decimal places such as 12.12345. On line 2, we use the "round" function to get a version of that number with just three decimal places, and display that. Note that this doesn't change the contents of "a", but if you needed to do that, you could simply assign the result from "round" back into the variable, e.g. with "a = round(a, 3)".

> ## ❓ CHALLENGE YOURSELF
>
> 1. At what point in a program should you put your function definitions?
> 2. What purpose do brackets serve in a function definition?
> 3. In a function definition called "test", which takes one numerical variable "a", how would you set "a" to be 10 by default, even if the calling program didn't specify a value?
> 4. What keyword do you use to send data back from a function to the calling code?
> 5. What is the difference between local and global variables?

05. Dealing with data

In this section

What are data structures?　56
Working with elements

The magic of tuples　57
Mixed items and slices

Lists and dictionaries　60
Changing elements on the fly
Sorting, adding and removing elements
Dictionaries
A practical example

Data and functions　67
Arbitrary numbers and parameters

Challenge yourself　69

As we progress through each section of this book, you're picking up the invaluable tools and techniques for creating, extending and maintaining Python programs. Variables, conditions, loops and functions are all essential elements of this, and the next thing to consider is data. Any program of any significance deals with data, whether it's a word processor (textual data), an image editor (pixel data) or a web browser (network data).

So far we've been working with simple data types in our code listings, namely numerical variables (like integers and floating-point numbers) along with text strings. These are very handy, but Python has some more sophisticated data structures that we can use. They allow us to work more efficiently with data, arrange it and sort it according to our needs – and we can also link pieces of data together like in a database.

DEALING WITH DATA
What are data structures?

Early on we talked about variables as storage spaces in memory where we can put data that changes often. When we use a variable to store a number, this is a very simple process – Python puts the number into an empty space in memory somewhere, and keeps track of its location using the variable's name. But what about text strings? These are slightly more complicated, because they are not just single items like numbers, but rather a series of smaller items: characters (letters, numbers and punctuation marks).

Consider this example. You write a Python program that, at the start, creates a variable called "x" that stores the number 100, and also a variable called "mystring" that contains the word "Hello". How does Python organize this in memory? Well, it could look something like this:

This is a simplified illustration of what happens inside your computer's memory, but it helps us to understand. In this case, when we create the "x" variable, Python finds a free space in memory to store the contents of "x" – and there just so happens to be free space at position 7162 in memory. (Think of your computer's memory, or RAM, as a sequence of empty storage spaces, each having a number from 1 up to however much memory you have installed.)

So from here onwards, whenever we need to use whatever's stored in the "x" variable, Python looks at location 7162 in the computer's memory. If we change the contents of "x" to a different number, Python puts that different number into 7162.

But what happens when we store a string in a variable? As mentioned, strings are actually sequences of characters, and multiple characters won't fit into a single space of memory. So instead, Python puts the string into multiple spaces – in this case, starting at position 7163. Our string is a structure of data starting from a specific point.

Working with elements

So now we know: "x" is stored at 7162, and "mystring" starts at 7163 (but uses multiple memory spaces). With this in mind, we can actually access the individual characters in a string, or "elements" as they're known, using square brackets like so:

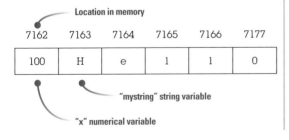

Location in memory

7162	7163	7164	7165	7166	7177
100	H	e	l	l	0

"mystring" string variable

"x" numerical variable

LISTING 46:

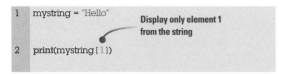

```
1   mystring = "Hello"
                                Display only element 1
                                from the string
2   print(mystring[1])
```

Up until this program, we have been printing strings in their entirety. This time, however, we have used square brackets to tell Python: just print element 1 from the string. So try running this program, and you'll see that it outputs the letter... "e".

What? Surely the first character/element in the string is "H", right? Well, not quite. In Python – as in many programming languages – elements in a data structure are counted from zero upwards. In the case of "Hello", "H" is element zero, "e" is element 1, the first "l" is element 2 and so forth. So to print "H", you would have to use "mystring[0]" instead.

So now we know that a string variable in Python is not just a single space in memory, but actually a sequence of

 Tip

You may find it daft and confusing that we count elements in strings (and other data structures) starting from zero. Why isn't the first element referred to with 1? There's a lot of history associated with this, and while some programming languages have broken the mold and count from 1 upwards, rather than zero, Python uses the "traditional" system. Just like with the nuances of human languages, you just have to get used to it – it soon becomes second nature. For more background on this topic, see **https://en.wikipedia.org/wiki/Zero-based_numbering**.

spaces – a data structure – all kept under the same variable name. Strings are rather simple structures, in that they're just linear sequences of characters, so let's move on to the more flexible data structures that Python offers.

The magic of tuples

A tuple is a structure that lets us group multiple pieces of data together under a single name. To create a tuple, we surround the data with brackets, and separate each piece of data – each element – using commas, like so:

LISTING 47:

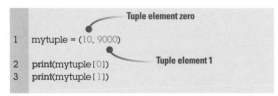

```
                            Tuple element zero

1   mytuple = (10, 9000)

                            Tuple element 1
2   print(mytuple[0])
3   print(mytuple[1])
```

Keeping in mind that elements in data structures are counted from zero upwards, you can probably guess what this program prints on the screen: 10 and 9000. But what makes tuples especially useful is that you can mix different types of data in them, such as numbers and text strings:

LISTING 48:

```
1   mytuple = (10, "awesome")
2   print(mytuple[0])
3   print(mytuple[1])
```

You may be starting to see the practical uses of tuples here, but let's look at a concrete example. Let's say you're working on a program that uses the days of the week. You don't want to hard-wire these names into the program – i.e. "Monday" every time the first day of the week comes up – because you may want to translate the program's interface into other languages.

One way to deal with this is to create string variables at the start of the program, so "day1" contains "Monday", "day2" contains "Tuesday" and so forth. In this way, your program can use those variables whenever it needs to display days, and the code doesn't care if you later change "Monday" to "Lundi" or "Montag" or anything else.

So far, so good. But now think about how you'd work with this data. Try creating a program where the user types a number of a day, and the program displays the name of that day. With the "day1", "day2" etc. variables we've outlined, it'd look like this:

LISTING 49:

```
1   day1 = "Monday"
2   day2 = "Tuesday"
3   day3 = "Wednesday"
4   day4 = "Thursday"
5
6   x = int(input("Enter a day number: "))
7
8   if x == 1:
9       print(day1)
10  elif x == 2:
11      print(day2)
12  elif x == 3:
13      print(day3)
14  elif x == 4:
15      print(day4)
```

To save space in the book, we haven't even implemented all days in this program – but even with just the first four, you can see that the code gets very repetitive. Wouldn't it make more sense to bundle all these days together into a tuple, so that we can access them under a single name, using elements for specific days? Listing 50 shows a tuple-based version of the previous program, but this time including all days, and it's much shorter as well!

In Listing 50, we use a tuple to store days of a week, and then access them via their element number.

Tip

You may notice in Listing 50 that we break up the contents of our tuple onto two lines. This is just to make it more readable in the book, and it's certainly valid Python. But when you're working on your own programs, it's usually best to keep everything on a single line, and let your text editor do the job of wrapping lines and making things easy to read.

LISTING 50:

```
1   days = ("Monday", "Tuesday", "Wednesday",
2   "Thursday", "Friday", "Saturday", "Sunday")
3
4   x = int(input("Enter a day number: "))
5
6   print("That day is", days[x-1])
```

That's much more elegant, isn't it? We don't need all the "if" statements; nor do we need a whole list of separate variables. We put everything together into a tuple and use the elements of it when we need them. Remember again that elements are counted from zero, hence the "x-1" on line 5: if the user types "1" for Monday, it's actually element zero in our tuple, so we subtract 1 from the number the user typed before getting the right element.

Mixed items and slices

As we mentioned, tuples can consist of mixed items: some elements can be numbers, and some can be text strings. And if we want to perform an operation on all elements in the tuple, we can use a "for" loop as we looked at earlier in the book, like so:

LISTING 51:

```
1   mytuple = (1, "Hello", 9000)
2
3   print(mytuple)
4                        Copy element from "mytuple" into
                         here during each loop
5   for x in mytuple:
6       print(x)
```

Before we look at the loop, a quick note about line 3: you'll see that it prints out all the tuple data, commas and quote marks included, just like we prepared it in line 1. This is just for you to see how Python stores the tuple. But that's not particularly useful in itself, so if we want to actually use the items contained in the tuple, without the additional formatting, we need to approach it in another way.

The "for" loop on lines 5 and 6 displays the elements on their own: the first time the loop executes, "x" contains element zero of the tuple, so the number 1 in this case. On the next iteration of the loop, "x" contains "Hello" and so on. The "for" loop ends when all elements of the tuple have been displayed – so the loop runs three times in this example.

Sometimes you may not want to perform a loop on all elements of a tuple, but rather a range of them. And sure enough, Python has a way to do that using "slices". Essentially, a slice is a selection of elements that can start or end at a specific place. Have a look at this code:

LISTING 52:

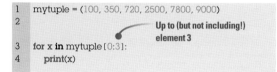

```
1   mytuple = (100, 350, 720, 2500, 7800, 9000)
2                              Up to (but not including!)
                               element 3
3   for x in mytuple [0:3]:
4       print(x)
```

Here we use a colon character inside our square brackets to specify a range: from element zero up to element 3 (so 4 elements in total). But Python only prints three numbers here – 100, 350 and 720!

So what's going on? Well, like with ranges in "for" loops, the final number in a slice merely says when the loop should end, not that it should be used in another iteration of the loop. So in this case, Python displays elements zero, 1 and 2 of the tuple, and when the "for" loop reaches element 3, it ends the loop and moves on to whatever's next.

The code in Listing 52 can be simplified slightly like so:

LISTING 53:

```
1   mytuple = (100, 350, 720, 2500, 7800, 9000)
2                              First 3 elements
3   for x in mytuple [:3]:
4       print(x)
```

In the square brackets on line 3 here, by omitting the start of the slice we tell Python to display the first three elements of the tuple (inclusive!) so the output is the same as before. If we changed "[:3]" to be "[3:]", then the loop would iterate over the last three numbers instead, so we'd see 2500, 7800 and 9000 on the screen.

One final thing about slices: they can be used on text strings as well as tuples, and they can take a third parameter which specifies how many elements to skip in each iteration of the loop. Let's look at this in action:

```
C:\Users\mike\Desktop\codingmanual>python
listing54.py
P
o
s
t
y
e
e

C:\Users\mike\Desktop\codingmanual>
```

Slices let us skip elements in strings and tuples – such as in Listing 54, where we only show certain characters in a text string.

LISTING 54:

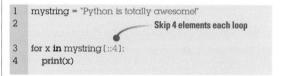

```
1   mystring = "Python is totally awesome!"
2                              Skip 4 elements each loop
3   for x in mystring [::4]:
4       print(x)
```

Here we've created a text string, where each element is a character. In the "for" loop on line 3, we don't specify a start or end – hence the lack of numbers around the colon characters – so Python will go through every element. But! The number 4 after the (unspecified) range tells Python to skip 4 elements after each iteration of the "for" loop. So the first iteration displays "P", the second "o", the third "s" and so on. Strings, tuples, slices and "for" loops are hugely powerful when used together, so try experimenting with different combinations and parameters.

Tip

A shorthand way to use the final element in a tuple, without having to know how many items are in the tuple, is to place -1 (negative 1) in the square brackets. For instance, if you have a tuple called "mytuple" with eight items, using "print(mytuple[-1])" will display the last element. Change that to -2 and you get the second-to-last element, and so on.

DEALING WITH DATA
Lists and dictionaries

Up until this point, there's one thing we haven't mentioned about tuples: their contents cannot be changed. You can't treat them like collections of variables, so code like this is simply not possible:

LISTING 55:

```
1   mytuple = (1, 2, 3)
2   mytuple[0] = 9000
```

Try to run this program, and Python will throw its arms in the air and tell you that the "tuple object does not support item assignment." In programming terms, we say that a tuple is "immutable." in that its state cannot be changed once it has been created. Now that you've discovered this, you may be wondering what the point of tuples is – after all, what's the point of a data structure if the data can't be changed?

Well, non-changing data like tuples can be processed extremely quickly by Python. But Python also has a very similar data structure called a list, which offers many of the same features as tuples but with the added ability to modify the data contained therein. In terms of appearance, the most notable difference is that lists are defined using square brackets, in contrast to the rounded ones of tuples:

LISTING 56:

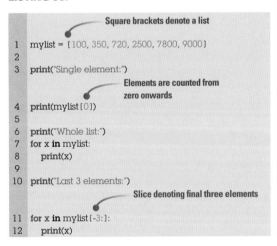

```
1    mylist = [100, 350, 720, 2500, 7800, 9000]
2
3    print("Single element:")
4    print(mylist[0])
5
6    print("Whole list:")
7    for x in mylist:
8        print(x)
9
10   print("Last 3 elements:")
11   for x in mylist[-3:]:
12       print(x)
```

Square brackets denote a list

Elements are counted from zero onwards

Slice denoting final three elements

Apart from the use of square brackets to define the list in line 1, most of the code here should now be familiar to you,

 A list within a list

You might be wondering if it's possible to embed one list inside another list – and yes, Python allows that. These "sublists" can be a bit tricky to work with, but they can also be very useful for managing complex types of data. To create a sublist (sometimes known as a "nested list") we use square brackets inside square brackets, like so:

LISTING 57:

```
1    mylist = [ [1, 2, 3], ["Bob", "Bill"] ]
2
3    print(mylist[0][2])
4    print(mylist[1][0])
5
6    for x in mylist[0]:
7        print(x)
```

In line 1 you can see that we start a list with an opening square bracket, but then we follow that with another opening square bracket for a sublist. This sublist contains 1, 2 and 3 – and then we close it with a square bracket before opening another list that contains "Bob" and "Bill".

Lines 3 and 4 demonstrate how to access individual elements of the sublists. In line 3, we tell Python: look inside sublist zero (i.e. the first sublist, as we count from zero as usual) and display element 2 (the third element, again counting from zero). This prints "3" on the screen. In line 4, we choose sublist number 1 (the second sublist) and element zero, which displays "Bob". Finally, on line 6 we use a "for" list to display all items in sublist zero, so we get "1", "2" and "3".

It's even possible to put sublists inside other sublists – but that's something for another day! Suffice to say, you may not use complicated data structures like these until you start writing advanced programs, but it's well worth being aware of them.

```
Command Prompt                          —    □    ×
C:\Users\mike\Desktop\codingmanual>python
listing56.py
Single element:
100
Whole list:
100
350
720
2500
7800
9000
Last 3 elements:
2500
7800
9000

C:\Users\mike\Desktop\codingmanual>
```

A list is a lot like a tuple, and you work with its elements in the same way. But with lists, you can also modify the elements.

based on the techniques we used with tuples. The "[-3:]" in the "for" loop on line 11 is a new trick: it's a slice of the final three items. If we didn't have the extra colon after it, Python would think we're referring to the third-to-last element, and not a slice, which makes no sense in a "for" loop so it would just show an error. So the colon is essential here to make it clear we want to iterate over a slice.

Changing elements on the fly

What should you do if you need to change an element in a list? You can simply use an assignment to place a value in the element, such as "mylist[3] = 20" to set element 3 of "mylist" to be 20. But in a loop, it's a bit more complicated, because you may not necessarily know which element in a list the loop is processing at any given moment.

Let's say you want to use a "for" loop to double all of the numbers in a list. You might be tempted to do something like this:

LISTING 58:

```
1    mylist = [20, 60, 500, 1200, 9000]
2
3    for x in mylist:
4        x = x * 2
5
6    print(mylist)
```

The problem here is, during each iteration of the "for" loop on line 3, the value of the current element in "mylist" is copied into the "x" variable. So on the first iteration of the

"for" loop, where "x" becomes 20, changing that "x" to something else has no effect on the actual contents of the list. That "x" is simply a stand-alone variable and takes on a new value with each iteration of the loop.

So we need to approach this in a different way. During the "for" loop, we need to change the actual contents of the list element being processed, and not just the throwaway "x" variable. To do this, we need to keep track of exactly which element in the list is being processed. Fortunately, Python has a rather neat "enumerate" function that helps in exactly this kind of scenario:

LISTING 59:

```
1    mylist = [20, 60, 500, 1200, 9000]
2
                 Variable that starts from zero and counts
                 up by 1 each loop iteration
3    for counter, x in enumerate(mylist):
4        print("Counter is:", counter)
5        print("x is:", x)
6        mylist[counter] = x * 2
7
8    print(mylist)
```

On line 3 here, we create a new "for" loop with a twist: we not only get the contents of the current "mylist" element into "x" with each iteration but we also use a variable we call "counter," which keeps track of how far through the list we've gone.

```
Command Prompt                          —    □    ×
C:\Users\mike\Desktop\codingmanual>python
listing59.py
Counter is: 0
x is: 20
Counter is: 1
x is: 60
Counter is: 2
x is: 500
Counter is: 3
x is: 1200
Counter is: 4
x is: 9000
[40, 120, 1000, 2400, 18000]

C:\Users\mike\Desktop\codingmanual>
```

In Listing 59, we use "for" and "enumerate" to work through a list, keeping track of which element we're processing, and doubling each element as we go. Then we show the results.

Look at it this way: when the loop starts and "enumerate" is run, "counter" contains 0 (for element zero of "mylist") and "x" contains 20. On the next iteration of the loop, "counter" contains 1 and "x" contains 60. On the next, "counter" contains 2 and "x" contains 500. And so on. So we're getting our values into "x" each iteration, but thanks to "counter" we can also keep track of exactly where we are in the list.

Lines 4 and 5 aren't necessary for the loop to function; they just show you what's going on when you run the program. Line 6 does the doubling magic: it multiplies the current value of "x" by 2, and places the result back into "mylist" at the appropriate place.

Sorting, adding and removing elements

After you've done lots of manipulation of a list, you may want to sort the data into a sensible order, especially if you're going to generate a report from it or save it onto the disk (more on that later in the book). This is really easy to do: just use the name of the list and add ".sort()" after it, like so:

LISTING 60:

```
1  mylist = [9000, 20, 500, 60, 1200]
2                    Sort the specified list numerically
3  mylist.sort()
4
5  for x in mylist:
6      print(x)
```

This rearranges the numbers inside "mylist" back into numerical order, as they were at the start of Listing 59. You can also use this special ".sort()" feature on string variables as well, but watch out! By default, Python gives priority to capital letters over lower-case letters. So if you have a list containing "My", "name", "is" and "Bill", and try to sort it using the same code as in Listing 60, Python will display them in this order: "Bill My is name".

Obviously "is" should come before "My" here, but as mentioned, capital letters get priority so Python puts them first. To remedy this, we need an extra bit of information in the ".sort()" code like so:

LISTING 61:

```
1  mylist = ["My", "name", "is", "Bill"]
2                    Do a case-insensitive
                     string sort
3  mylist.sort(key=str.lower)
4
5  for x in mylist:
6      print(x)
```

Tip

Want to sort a list in reverse order, so that the largest numbers come first, or the strings are sorted from Z to A? Just add a "reverse=True" parameter inside the ".sort()" bit of code. With strings, you can even combine that with the case-insensitive search option we used in Listing 61 by separating the parameters inside the brackets with a comma: "key=str.lower, reverse=True".

The "key=str.lower" addition in line 3 here tells Python to sort without regards to upper or lower-case – so the results are "Bill is My name" as expected.

Adding elements to a list and removing them is nice and easy. To add something to the end, we simply use the list name followed by ".append()", with the item inside the brackets, like so:

LISTING 62:

```
1  mylist = [20, 60, 500, 1200, 9000]
2                    Add this element to end of the list
3  mylist.append(10)
4  print(mylist)
```

You can use this ".append()" feature to not only add extra stand-alone items to a list but also to add another list as well. Be careful, though: if you use ".append()" with a list inside the brackets, it will be included as a sublist. To simply extend the contents of one list with the contents of another, we use ".extend()", e.g. "mylist. extend(myotherlist)". In this case, all items in "myotherlist" are added onto the end of "mylist".

In many scenarios, you won't just want to tack an item on to the end of a list, but rather place it in a certain position. For this we can use ".insert()", which has two parameters: the location in the list, and the element data to add. Here's how it works:

LISTING 63:

```
1  mylist = [20, 60, 500, 1200, 9000]
2                    Position – insert before this element
3  mylist.insert(1, 10)
4  print(mylist)      Element data to insert
```

Once again, don't forget that we count from zero with elements in lists and tuples. So in line 3 here, we tell Python to insert the value 10 before element 1, i.e. the second element in the list (60). The result here is that the list then contains 20, 10, 60, 500 and so forth.

To remove items, we have a couple of features at our disposal. We can tell Python to search for a specific value in a list, and remove the first instance it sees of it. Consider this code:

LISTING 64:

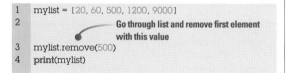

```
1   mylist = [20, 60, 500, 1200, 9000]
2                          Go through list and remove first element
                           with this value
3   mylist.remove(500)
4   print(mylist)
```

After this, the list contains 20, 60, 1200 and 9000. But what if the list contains multiple 500s, and you want to remove them all? You could just copy and paste the "remove" code, but if you're working with a very long list and you're not sure how many elements containing 500 are in there, you'd be a bit stumped.

Fortunately, there's a solution. (Indeed, there are multiple solutions, as is often the case in Python, but here we'll focus on a simple and straightforward one.) Using "mylist.count(x)", where "x" is the value we want to search for, we can find out how many instances of "x" are in the list. Then we can use that number in a "for" loop combined with a range to work through the list until all instances have been removed. Let's take the list from Listing 64, add a few more 500s to it, and see how this works:

LISTING 65:

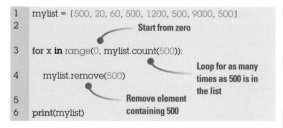

```
1   mylist = [500, 20, 60, 500, 1200, 500, 9000, 500]
2                          Start from zero
3   for x in range(0, mylist.count(500)):
                               Loop for as many
                               times as 500 is in
4       mylist.remove(500)     the list
5                      Remove element
6   print(mylist)      containing 500
```

You will recall the range feature from earlier in the book, which gives a "for" loop a set of numbers to iterate over. In this case, we tell "for" to run the loop for as many times as "mylist.count(500)" returns – in other words, for as many times as 500 appears in the list. Then, on line 4, we remove the element in each iteration of the loop. So the end result is that all 500s get removed.

To remove an element based on its position in the list, rather than its contents, we can use ".pop()". This also tells us what the element contained before it was removed, which can be useful if we want to do something else with it. Let's see this in action – and make it interactive:

LISTING 66:

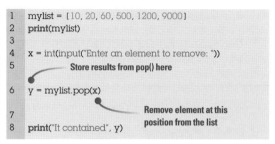

```
1   mylist = [10, 20, 60, 500, 1200, 9000]
2   print(mylist)
3
4   x = int(input("Enter an element to remove: "))
5                  Store results from pop() here
6   y = mylist.pop(x)
                              Remove element at this
7                             position from the list
8   print("It contained", y)
```

So here, we start off with a list as usual. We then get the user to enter a number corresponding to a position in the list, and then remove the element at that position – "popping" it off the list. But, we also store its old value in our "y" variable, which we can then use later. So when you run this program, if you enter 0 (zero) it'll display 10, which is element zero in the list. If you enter 1, you'll see 20, and so on.

> **ℹ Tip**
>
> Want to find the position in a list where a number or string appears for the first time? Use the ".index(x)" feature, where "x" is the thing you're searching for. As an example, if you have a list called "mylist" containing 10, 20, 30, 40 and 50, and do "a = mylist.index(30)", the "a" variable will then contain 2 – as 30 is at position 2 in the list, counting from zero.

Dictionaries

We've seen how tuples and lists are very useful ways of grouping together bits of data under a single name. But both of these data types have a limitation: you need to refer to the individual elements in them using numbers. This is fine in many cases, but wouldn't it be more useful if each item had its own name?

This is where Python's dictionaries come into play. They're a lot like tuples and lists, but we can provide custom names for elements and then refer to specific elements using those names – instead of mere numbers. Let's take an example using employees in a company, along with their telephone extension numbers. In the first line of this code, we create a dictionary where each name has a number:

LISTING 67:

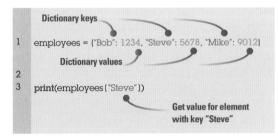

```
1    employees = {"Bob": 1234, "Steve": 5678, "Mike": 9012}

2
3    print(employees["Steve"])
```

Dictionary keys

Dictionary values

Get value for element with key "Steve"

To create a dictionary, we use curly brackets. Inside these we put pairs of "keys" and "values", joined together by colon (:) characters. The keys are what we use to refer to the elements in the dictionary, and the values are their data. So line 1 of Listing 67 creates a dictionary with three elements called "Bob", "Steve" and "Mike". They contain the values 1234, 5678 and 9012 respectively. (Note that dictionaries can contain mixed data with numbers and strings – the latter need to be surrounded by double quote marks as usual.)

On line 3, we tell Python to print one of the elements in the dictionary. But, unlike with tuples or lists, we don't need to specify a number for the element here. Instead, we can provide a name, which is much more useful and easy to work with for many types of data. So when we tell Python to display the "employee" dictionary element called "Steve", it searches through the dictionary until it finds that element and then prints the number matched with it – so 5678 in this case.

Let's look at some more operations that we can perform on dictionaries. Like with lists, we can change the data

 Tip

Here we're using strings as key names in our dictionaries, but you can also use numbers (omitting the double quote marks) as keys. Note that key names have to be unique, however – if you end up with a list that contains multiple items sharing the same key name, your program will almost certainly end up containing bugs that are difficult to debug.

contained in them, remove elements and add new ones, as we show in Listing 68:

LISTING 68:

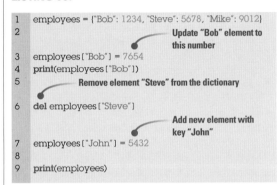

```
1    employees = {"Bob": 1234, "Steve": 5678, "Mike": 9012}
2
3    employees["Bob"] = 7654
4    print(employees["Bob"])
5
6    del employees["Steve"]
7    employees["John"] = 5432
8
9    print(employees)
```

Update "Bob" element to this number

Remove element "Steve" from the dictionary

Add new element with key "John"

Here we create the same dictionary as in Listing 67, but on line 3 we change the number stored in the element that has the key "Bob". On line 6, we remove the "Steve"

element from the dictionary, and on line 7 we tell Python to add a new element with a key of "John" and value of 5432. The final line of code here displays the dictionary – showing both its keys and values – so you can see the end result with items "Bob", "John" and "Mike".

To find out if a dictionary contains a specific element, we can use the "in" keyword in combination with a dictionary name and key. This allows us to start building more advanced programs, such as in Listing 69 where we take input from the user to get an employee name, and then display the corresponding phone number:

LISTING 69:

```
1  employees = {"Bob": 1234, "Steve": 5678, "Mike": 9012}
2
3  text = ""
4
5  while text != "q":
6      text = input("Enter a name, or 'q' to quit: ")
7
            Does "employees" dictionary contain key
            name in "text" variable?
8      if(text in employees):
            Do this if so
9          print(employees[text])
10     else:
11         print("Not found")
```

Here we start a loop on line 5 that takes input from the user, and ends the loop (and program) when "q" alone is entered. If the user enters a name (case-sensitive), we check line 8 to see if it matches a key in the "employees" dictionary, using the aforementioned "in" keyword. If the key is found, if the user enters "Bob", "Steve" or "Mike", then the corresponding value is displayed. Otherwise the program prints a "Not found" message.

A practical example

Given everything we've learned so far, we can now build a useful little employee directory program, like in Listing 70. One thing we don't know how to do yet is load and save data from the disk – but we're covering that later in the book. For now, we create a couple of "stub" load and save functions that don't do anything, but remind us that we need to fill them in with working code later. (Using "XXX" to denote things that need attention is common in coding – it makes it easy to search for these things in your editor.)

So here's our fully functional (apart from loading/saving) program. We print a welcome message, ask a user to enter a single-letter command, and then perform the appropriate operation:

LISTING 70:

```
1  def load_data(filename):
2      print("XXX NOT IMPLEMENTED")
            Stub function – to be implemented later
3
4  def save_data(filename):
5      print("XXX NOT IMPLEMENTED")
6
7  employees = {"Bob": 1234, "Steve": 5678, "Mike": 9012}
8  text = ""
9
10 while text != "q":
            New line (\n) character to jump to start of
            next line
11     print("\n--- Employee Directory Tool 1.0 ---")
            Simple user interface, showing available
            commands
12     print("Enter 'f' to find, 'a' to add, 'd' to delete,")
13     print("'l' to load, 's' to save, 'q' to quit")
14     text = input("Your option: ")
15
            Find an employee and display
            his/her number
16     if(text == 'f'):
17         text = input("Enter name: ")
18         if(text in employees):
19             print("Number:", employees[text])
20         else:
21             print("Not found")
            Add a new employee and number
            to the dictionary
23     elif(text == 'a'):
24         text = input("Enter new name: ")
25         num = int(input("Enter number: "))
26         employees[text] = num
27
            Delete an employee from the
            dictionary
28     elif(text == 'd'):
29         text = input("Enter name: ")
30         if(text in employees):
31             del employees[text]
32         else:
33             print("Not found")
34
35     elif(text == 'l'):
36         text = input("Enter filename to load: ")
37         load_data(text)
38
39     elif(text == 's'):
40         text = input("Enter filename to save: ")
41         save_data(text)
```

Phew – that's our longest program yet! But it's also the most practical, demonstrating many of the things we've covered in a real-world scenario. You should be able to understand it, but there are a couple of things we'll note.

```
Command Prompt - python listing70.py                    —   □   ✕

--- Employee Directory Tool 1.0 ---
Enter 'f' to find, 'a' to add, 'd' to delete,
'l' to load, 's' to save, 'q' to quit
Your option: a
Enter new name: Kevin
Enter number: 9876

--- Employee Directory Tool 1.0 ---
Enter 'f' to find, 'a' to add, 'd' to delete,
'l' to load, 's' to save, 'q' to quit
Your option: f
Enter name: Mike
Number: 9012

--- Employee Directory Tool 1.0 ---
Enter 'f' to find, 'a' to add, 'd' to delete,
'l' to load, 's' to save, 'q' to quit
Your option:
```

With Listing 70, we're using some of the skills and techniques we've learned so far in a proper program that could be extended for real-world usage.

Firstly, if we had the ability to load and save files, we'd probably ask the user for a file name at the beginning. But because we're missing this (at the moment!), we set up the dictionary inside the code itself on line 7.

Then we start a "while" loop on line 10, printing some information text as a simple user interface. Note the "\n" bit with the backslash on line 11 – this simply represents a newline character, so it provides a bit of spacing in the interface. Each time the loop runs, it displays the help text, so the extra blank line breaks things up a bit on the screen and makes the program output more readable.

The following "if" and "elif" code chunks use the techniques we practiced earlier to search for, add and remove items from the dictionary. The final two "elif" bits handle file loading and saving, and we even use "input" to get the file name, thereby completing the main code. All we have to do later is fill in the code for the "load_data" and "save_data" routines – we don't need to add more to the main code. This is modularity in action, as we've talked about before.

So try running this program – you can search for employees (case-sensitive), add new ones and delete existing ones. We've kept the user interface and input text short for the book, but you could add more informative feedback and error messages.

ⓘ Looping through dictionaries

In some cases, you may want to perform a loop on dictionaries, going through the items and getting the key name and value for each one. This is simple enough to do using a "for" loop, adding "items()" to the dictionary name and getting the results back into two variables, like so:

LISTING 71:

```
1   employees = {"Bob": 1234, "Steve": 5678, "Mike": 9012}
2
3   for name, number in employees.items():
4       print("Call", name, "on", number)
```

This "for" loop on line 3 simply iterates through all items in the dictionary, getting the key into the "name" variable and value into "number". So the first time this loop runs, "name" contains "Bob" and "number" contains 1234. For the second iteration, "name" contains "Steve" and "number" contains 5678 – and so forth.

DEALING WITH DATA
Data and functions

Earlier in the book, when we were looking at functions, we saw how it's possible to get data back from a function. Listing 36 shows an example of this in action using the "return" keyword. For many functions that you create, they will only need to send back one piece of data – such as a file name or error number. But as you create more intricate programs you may need a function to accept or return varying amounts of data, and that's what we'll explore now.

The simplest way for a function to return multiple pieces of data is to separate them with commas, as we do in Listing 72:

LISTING 72:

```
1    def my_func():
2        return 50, 9000
3
4    x, y = my_func()
5
6    print(x)
7    print(y)
```

The "return" on line 2 here sends back two values, 50 and 9000, and in line 4 these are placed into the "x" and "y" variables respectively. You can, of course, add more return values and variables as you wish – it all depends on exactly what your program is trying to achieve.

But what if you have lots of values to return from a function? Using separate variables can become tiresome, especially if you're only using them temporarily and have to keep inventing new names for them! Fortunately, this is where our good friend the tuple comes back into play. A function can return a series of values inside brackets, turning them into a tuple, which can be accessed by the calling code under a single name. That's what we do here:

LISTING 73:

```
1    def my_func():
                         Brackets make the return value a tuple
2        return (50, 9000, 200)
3
4    mytuple = my_func()
5
6    print(mytuple[0])
7    print(mytuple[1])
8    print(mytuple[2])
```

So on line 2 here, by placing the return values inside brackets, we bundle them together into a single data type – a tuple. This means we can access everything inside it using a single line, as we do on line 4, and then on lines 6 to 8 we access the individual elements of the tuple using the square brackets (remembering, once again, that zero refers to the first element in the tuple – 50 in this case).

Bear in mind that tuples can't be changed, as we discussed earlier, so if you want to modify the returned data, it's better to use a list instead. And as we've seen, tuples and lists share pretty much the same characteristics otherwise – so in Listing 73, you can change the tuple on line 2 into a list simply by replacing the round brackets with square ones. (And you'd probably want to change the name on line 4 to "mylist" or something, just to avoid confusion.)

So functions can return single values, multiple values specified separately, or tuples, lists and even dictionaries. Keeping in mind variable scope as we talked about before, so that variables inside a function don't tread on global variables used elsewhere, you can now create advanced functions that process and return a lot of data, all nicely modular and never interfering with the main program code. There's something else we can do with functions and data though.

Arbitrary numbers of parameters

Every function we've created so far takes a specific number of parameters in the definition. Look back at Listing 32: it takes one parameter, "name". Listing 34 takes two parameters, "x" and "y". For most of your programming work, you'll know exactly what a function needs to do and how many parameters it should take. However, it's often useful if a function can take a varying number of parameters – sometimes one, sometimes a few, sometimes ten or more.

For instance, consider a function that takes a series of numbers and returns the average of them. The code that calls the function may sometimes want to send just a handful of numbers to the function, or other times a larger data set. By using the arbitrary parameter length marker, denoted by an asterisk (*) symbol, we can write a function that happily accepts varying amounts of parameters. Here we can see it in action:

LISTING 74:

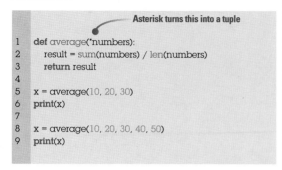

Asterisk turns this into a tuple

```
1   def average(*numbers):
2       result = sum(numbers) / len(numbers)
3       return result
4
5   x = average(10, 20, 30)
6   print(x)
7
8   x = average(10, 20, 30, 40, 50)
9   print(x)
```

You can see here that we only have one parameter in our "average" function, called "numbers", but by placing the asterisk before it, we turn it into a tuple reference. So all of the numbers passed to the function – regardless of how many – are placed into the tuple. On line 2, we generate an average of those numbers by using a couple of built-in routines: we take the sum of all numbers in the tuple, and then divide them by the length of the tuple (i.e. how many elements it contains). Finally, on line 3 we return that result back to the calling code.

On lines 5 and 8, you can see that we call our "average" function twice, each time with a different number of parameters. Thanks to the tuple reference, the function doesn't get confused by this and happily does its work. But what about scenarios when you want to pass a tuple or list to a function, instead of separate values like we do in lines 5 and 8 here?

To do this, you can't just send the tuple or list as a parameter – this will confuse Python mightily, as the function expects a distinct series of numbers. Instead, we have to use an asterisk symbol again, but this time in the calling code. Let's see how this works in Listing 75:

LISTING 75:

```
1   def average(*numbers):
2       result = sum(numbers) / len(numbers)
3       return result
4
5   mytuple = (10, 20, 30)
```

Unpack tuple items before sending them to the function

```
6   x = average(*mytuple)
7   print(x)
8
9   mylist = [10, 20, 30, 40, 50]
10  x = average(*mylist)
11  print(x)
```

 Tip

Hopefully at this point, you're starting to feel quite at home with Python's structure and syntax. Some things may be irking you though, like the way symbols are occasionally reused for different purposes. We've already seen that an asterisk (*) can denote multiplication, arbitrary function parameters and tuple/list unpacking, for instance. Why the duplication? Couldn't the Python designers have used something else like a big "MULTIPLY" keyword? That would have been possible, but it would arguably make the code look rather ugly. Ultimately, the context makes it clear what each symbol does, so it becomes second nature what it's doing. It's much like in human languages, where words and sounds can have very different meanings depending on context and position in a sentence, but we understand them (most of the time).

The asterisks on lines 6 and 9 here tell Python to expand or "unpack" the tuple and list into individual items before sending them to the function. This is essential because the function expects individual numbers, and not another data type. Without the asterisks you'd get an "unsupported operand type(s)" message from Python and the program wouldn't work – but with the asterisks, everything is clear, both to the developer and to the hard-working Python interpreter.

? **CHALLENGE YOURSELF**

1. If the string variable "mystring" contains "Hello", how would you refer to the element containing the letter "o"?
2. What are the differences between tuples and lists?
3. If "mylist" is a list of names and you want to sort it case-insensitively, what would you do?
4. If you have a dictionary called "employees", how do you remove the item with the key "Bob"?
5. How would you define a function called "summary" which takes an arbitrary number of values in "data"?

06.

Saving your results

In this section

Saving data to files   72
Tips and tricks for saving

Reading text and binary   75
Working with structured data
Reading binary files

Searching through files   79
Finding and changing your position

Handling Python data   82
The JSON alternative

Challenge yourself   85

Back in the early 1980s, many home computers weren't supplied with any way to load or store data. Once you took the machine out of the box, you had to type in manually any program or game you wanted to run – usually from a listing in a book or magazine. For small programs, this wasn't much of a hassle; and indeed, typing in programs by hand is a good way to learn a programming language, as we suggested earlier in this book.

But ultimately, every serious computer user needed some way to store data permanently. For those old 8-bit computers, cassette players were normally used – and some computers eventually had them built in, like the awesome ZX Spectrum +2. These cassettes were, of course, superseded by floppy drives, and then along came CD-RWs, SD cards and USB keys.

Anyway, most programs beyond simple demos and games need some way to load and store data, and that's what we'll be looking at in this section. As you may have come to expect from Python by now, the language is loaded with useful routines and features to make this a fairly straightforward process.

SAVING YOUR RESULTS
Saving data to files

We've worked with data in the form of strings and numerical variables before – but how do we save this data into a file on the disk? You may remember the "Fun with built-in functions" subsection earlier in this book, but one that we didn't include there is "open". This is Python's function for accessing files, and it's really easy to use. All we need to do is specify a file name, along with the mode for opening the file.

We set this mode using a single character parameter: "r" to read data, "w" to write data (overwriting the original if the file already exists), and "a" to append data onto the end of an existing file. Listing 76 shows us how this works:

LISTING 76:

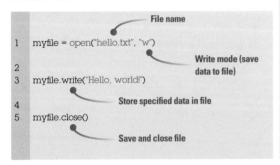

```
1    myfile = open("hello.txt", "w")

2
3    myfile.write("Hello, world!")

4
5    myfile.close()
```

File name

Write mode (save data to file)

Store specified data in file

Save and close file

Pretty straightforward, right? On line 1, we open a file called "hello.txt" – if this doesn't exist, Python creates it from scratch as a blank file. If it does exist, however, it's opened and all existing data is removed from it, so that we can write new data to it. The "open" here returns a file object, which we store in "myfile". Objects are a topic that we cover later in the book, but they are like super turbocharged variables that have extra facilities. So for now, just think of "myfile" (or whatever name you use for your file objects) as a way to refer to a specific file that you've opened.

On line 3, we use "write" to tell our "myfile" object that we want to store some data in it. And just like in a typical "print" command, we specify what we want to store in brackets and double quotation marks. So in this case, we store the text "Hello, world!" in the file. We're not quite done yet, though – it's important that we tell Python that we've finished with this file, and want to make sure all the data is fully saved and that the file closed. So we do that on line 5, and after this, we can't do anything else with the "myfile" object without opening it again.

Run this program, and although there will be no output on the screen, you'll see in your file manager that a "hello.txt" file appears alongside the code. Have a look at it inside your text editor, and it'll show "Hello, world!" as expected. There we have it – data saved to a file, in just three lines of code!

Dealing with file errors

In Listing 76, we created the "hello.txt" file in the same folder (aka directory) as the program itself, so we should have write permission there – in other words, we should be allowed to save files there as a normal user. But what happens if you try to save a file in a location that's not allowed? The administrator (or "root") user on your operating system can change files everywhere, but when you're logged in as your normal user account, there's a limit to the things you can change. This is to stop malware and other dubious programs trying to infect critical system files.

To see how this works, make sure you're logged in as your normal user account, and then alter the file name on line 1 of Listing 76: if you're on Windows, change it to "C:\Windows\hello.txt" – and for macOS or Linux, use "/hello.txt" (forward slash at the beginning). In both of these cases, we're changing our program so that it tries to save a file in a location that normal users cannot touch: the special C:\Windows folder in Windows, or the root (/) folder in other operating systems. Now, when you run the code, it will halt execution on line 1 with a "Permission denied" error.

That's good – it stops our program from trying to do any damage. But often you don't want the program to simply terminate at this stage, but rather handle the error itself and continue. We can do this using a technique called "exception handling," and it looks like this:

LISTING 77:

```
1    try:
2        myfile = open("C:\Windows\hello.txt", "w")
3    except OSError as err:
4        print(err)
5
6    print("Moving on...")
```

This is for Windows – change the filename to "/hello.txt" on macOS or Linux as mentioned. The "try" and "except" bits here, with their indented code, help us to trap the error without terminating the program. Python tries the "open" code in line 2, and, if it works, jumps down to the next main code on line 6. If the file can't be opened, however, an "OSError" is generated, and we handle that ourselves on line 3. We get the exact error message into "err" and display it, before carrying on with the code on line 6.

With this technique, you can try to perform file operations and then handle them gracefully if they fail, without Python just closing the whole program. For instance, you could ask the user for another file name, or ask them to plug in an external device if you're saving data there.

```
Command Prompt                    —    □    ×

C:\Users\mike\Desktop\codingmanual>python
listing76.py

C:\Users\mike\Desktop\codingmanual>type
hello.txt
Hello, world!
C:\Users\mike\Desktop\codingmanual>
```

Using the "type'"command on Windows (or "cat' on macOS and Linux) we can look at what's inside "hello.txt" after running Listing 76.

Tips and tricks for saving

Note that the "write" function we're using simply saves data as a stream of characters to a file – it doesn't pay any attention to formatting. So look at what happens when you do this:

LISTING 78:

```
1    myfile = open("hello.txt", "w")
2
3    myfile.write("Hello, world!")
4    myfile.write("We're learning coding.")
5    myfile.write("Pretty cool, right?")
6
7    myfile.close()
```

You may expect lines 3, 4 and 5 here to add separate lines to our "hello.txt" file, but actually all the data ends up

Inside Coding

bundled together: "Hello, world! We're learning coding. Pretty cool, right?" To fix this, we can add the newline (\n) character that we came across a bit earlier in the book. Add these to the end of each text string we want to save on lines 3, 4 and 5 – i.e. before the final quotation marks – and run the program again. This time, each "write" operation stores the text on a separate line.

Using the "close" function after writing to a file is important, but what about if you're juggling lots of open files across a long section of code, and aren't sure which ones need to be closed at certain points? There's a very Pythonesque solution to this, and it uses – as you may have guessed by now – indented code blocks. It looks like this:

LISTING 79:

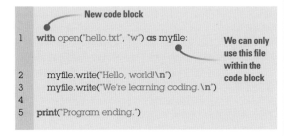

```
     New code block
1   with open("hello.txt", "w") as myfile:        We can only
                                                   use this file
                                                   within the
2       myfile.write("Hello, world!\n")            code block
3       myfile.write("We're learning coding.\n")
4
5   print("Program ending.")
```

On line 1 here, we open our file as usual, but by placing it after a "with" keyword and adding "as myfile" and a colon afterwards, we set up "myfile" to be used inside the following indented code. "myfile" will only exist for the lifespan of the indented code block – much like the local variables we explored earlier in the book. So on lines 2 and 3 we write some data to the file, but then the code block ends. What happens here? Python automatically closes the

```
Command Prompt                          —  □  ×

C:\Users\mike\Desktop\codingmanual>python
listing79.py
Program ending.

C:\Users\mike\Desktop\codingmanual>type
hello.txt
Hello, world!
We're learning coding.

C:\Users\mike\Desktop\codingmanual>
```

The "hello.txt" generated by Listing 79 has two lines of text – and we use a different technique to open the file, so we don't need to close it manually.

file before carrying on with execution on line 5. As soon as the indentation stops and the code block ends, we can't access "myfile" any more (unless we re-open it of course).

ℹ **Tip**

If you want to write data onto the end of an existing file, without its contents being removed first, use "a" (append) as the write mode parameter when calling "open". To try this out, edit Listing 79 so that the "w" on the first line is "a", and then run the program a few times. When you now have a peek inside the "hello. txt" file, you'll see that each time the program was run, it kept adding lines on to the end of the file.

SAVING YOUR RESULTS
Reading text and binary

Now that we have saving data out of the way, let's look at how to load data from the disk. The actual process of accessing a file is very similar, and we can handle errors (like missing files) gracefully by using the "try" and "except" feature described in the "Dealing with file errors" box earlier in this section. Here's how to access a file for reading data:

LISTING 80:

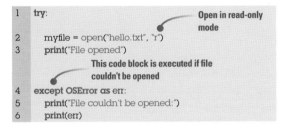

```
1   try:                                    Open in read-only
                                            mode
2       myfile = open("hello.txt", "r")
3       print("File opened")
                        This code block is executed if file
                        couldn't be opened
4   except OSError as err:
5       print("File couldn't be opened:")
6       print(err)
```

So if you have a "hello.txt" file alongside the code for this program and run it, you should see the "File opened" message. Try changing the file name in line 2 to something that doesn't exist, however, and you'll see that our exception handler, starting on line 4, springs into action. All together, here we have a sensible way of opening a file for reading data, with a fallback in case something goes wrong.

Let's now look at how to pull data out of a file and use it. For this example, make sure that "hello.txt" contains a few lines of text – it doesn't matter what. Just tap in three or four lines of text that can be used by the program in Listing 81:

LISTING 81:

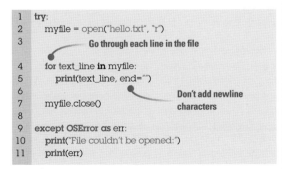

```
1   try:
2       myfile = open("hello.txt", "r")
3                Go through each line in the file
4       for text_line in myfile:
5           print(text_line, end="")
6
7       myfile.close()          Don't add newline
                                 characters
8
9   except OSError as err:
10      print("File couldn't be opened:")
11      print(err)
```

Here we open the "hello.txt" file in read-only mode, and then start a "for" loop on line 4. This loop simply works its way through every line of text in the file, placing each line

---

ⓘ Reading whole files at once

In Listing 81, we process a text file my creating a "myfile" object and pulling our lines from it in a "for" loop, one-by-one. What options are available if you want to read an entire file in one fell swoop, however? Add a bunch of lines of random text to "hello.txt", and then try the following:

LISTING 82:

```
1   text_data = open("hello.txt", "r").read()
2
3   print(text_data)
```

The extra ".read()" on the end of line 1 here tells Python to read all data from the file and place it into the "text_data" string variable. This is the raw data, so it includes newline characters and others that are not visible in the normal text sense. Additionally, once Python has read the file in this way, it closes the file automatically so you don't have to.

If you want to read a whole file at once, but need to break up the data into separate lines, that's possible as well. To achieve this, change ".read()" in line 1 of Listing 82 to ".readlines()", which returns a list instead of a simple text string. You can then go through the list like so:

LISTING 83:

```
1   text_list = open("hello.txt", "r").readlines()
2
3   for line in text_list:
4       print(line, end="")
```

So once line 1 has been executed here, "text_list" is a list containing all the lines from the file. Therefore "text_list[0]" contains the first line, "text_list[1]" contains the second, and so on. Using a "for" loop we can iterate over all lines in the file, printing them in this case (and adding the "end" parameter to "print" to avoid printing extra newline characters on top of those already in the file).

into the "text_line" variable for each iteration of the loop. So if "hello.txt" contains three lines of text, this loop will run three times – first with line 1 of text, then with line 2 and then with line 3.

Note the extra "end" parameter in our "print" function call; we used this way back in Listing 42, to stop "print" from adding a newline character after every line it displays. Because the text file already includes newline characters, we don't need "print" to add its own here (otherwise we'd have double spacing – try removing the "end" parameter to see).

Working with structured data

If your programs only need to work with simple lines of plain text, then congratulations – you now have all the tools and skills required! But sometimes you'll need to process more structured data, plucking out the pieces you need whilst ignoring the rest. Let's take the venerable comma separated value (CSV) format, which is often used for exchanging data between different spreadsheet programs. In a CSV file, each line is like a row in a spreadsheet, and each column is separated by commas.

Let's go back to our employee directory example. Create a new text file called "data.txt", in the same folder as your Python programs, and place the following in it:

```
Mike, 1234
Bob, 4567
Steve, 8910
```

So that's three lines, each containing a name and an extension number, separated by commas. This is a simple CSV file – and now we'll explore how to process it in your Python code.

We want our program to read this file, go through each line, and for each line get the two bits of information (the name and the number). We can do this by splitting the line

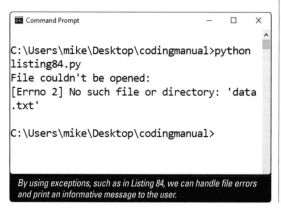

```
C:\Users\mike\Desktop\codingmanual>python
listing84.py
File couldn't be opened:
[Errno 2] No such file or directory: 'data
.txt'

C:\Users\mike\Desktop\codingmanual>
```

By using exceptions, such as in Listing 84, we can handle file errors and print an informative message to the user.

where there's a comma, which gives us the results in the form of a list. Then we can use the contents of this list to populate the "employee" dictionary. Sounds tough? It's actually pretty quick to do, as you can see in Listing 84:

LISTING 84:

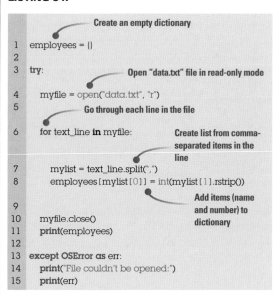

```
1   employees = {}
2
3   try:
4       myfile = open("data.txt", "r")
5
6       for text_line in myfile:
7           mylist = text_line.split(",")
8           employees[mylist[0]] = int(mylist[1].rstrip())
9
10      myfile.close()
11      print(employees)
12
13  except OSError as err:
14      print("File couldn't be opened:")
15      print(err)
```

Here we create an empty dictionary and then open the "data. txt" file we created beforehand. On line 6, we start a "for" loop which iterates over every line in the file. Each time a line is processed, we perform a "split" operation on line 7: this splits the contents of "text_line" into multiple parts, based on where it finds commas, and returns the results as a list.

When line 7 is processing "Mike, 1234" in the "text_line" variable, the "split" operation places "Mike" into "mylist[0]" (the first item in the list), and 1234 into "mylist[1]". The comma itself is discarded by the "split" operation. That's all well and good – we've managed to read the data and parse it into a more structured format than just plain text.

What's next? On line 8, we populate our dictionary by placing the name (key) and number (value) in it. As you saw earlier, to add items to a dictionary we just provide the key and value – we don't need to perform any specific insertion function. So on the first iteration of the loop, we add "mylist[0]" ("Mike") to the dictionary as a key, and "mylist[1]" (1234) as its value, converting it from a text string to a proper integer number using "int".

Note the "rstrip()" operation for the value here – this removes excess data (such as newline characters) from the end of the number. We don't really need to do this, as Python is clever enough to pluck the numeric value out of

Tip

Thanks to the "split", as used on line 7 of Listing 84, we can process many other types of data as well. For instance, a common alternative to comma-separated files are tab-separated files. Edit "data.txt" and instead of using a comma to separate the names and numbers, hit the tab key instead. Then edit line 7 and change the "," part in "split" to be '\t' (backslash-t). This tells Python to split the data whenever it comes across a tab character, so you'll get the same results. As you've seen, "\t" and "\n" are useful ways of representing characters that aren't usually visible in text files, but add spacing.

the string and ignore extra fluff, but it's just good practice to clean up data before you use it.

Anyway, when the "for" loop has completed, all three lines of the file have been processed and our dictionary is populated. We finish off by closing the file and displaying the dictionary contents on the screen, so you can see if it has worked correctly. This is a really practical example of using Python to parse plain text files into usable data formats for processing, and you can elaborate on it in your own programs.

Reading binary files

While text files are great for reading, processing and storing human-readable data, in some situations you may need to work with binary data as well. This is data as the computer sees it – a series of numbers – which doesn't usually make sense to our human eyes. For instance, consider an image on a website: it's a file made up of hundreds or thousands of numbers describing the color of each dot, how wide the image is, how many colors are used, and so on. Your web browser reads the binary data in the image file, processes it, and converts it into the right sequence of dots on the screen.

Image files could theoretically be created in human-readable text, with zillions of lines like "Place a red dot at coordinates X and Y," but that would be enormously wasteful and time-consuming. Hence binary is used instead. In your web browser, go to any site and save a small image to your hard drive (right-click and choose "Save as"). Save it alongside your Python programs as "image.dat" – we don't care about the extension or file format in this case. Just make sure the image is smaller than 100KB, so it doesn't take too long for Python to process!

Next, enter and run the following program:

LISTING 85:

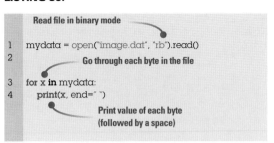

```
   Read file in binary mode
1  mydata = open("image.dat", "rb").read()
2             Go through each byte in the file
3  for x in mydata:
4      print(x, end=" ")
              Print value of each byte
              (followed by a space)
```

In this case, we open the file in "rb" (read binary) mode, and then iterate over each byte of it using a "for" loop. But what is a byte? It's the simplest way of representing an individual piece of data from a file. A byte can contain values between 0 and 255 – and from there, 1024 bytes is a kilobyte, 1024 kilobytes is a megabyte, and 1024 megabytes is a gigabyte.

So if the image file you downloaded is exactly 3 kilobytes (KB), it will contain 3 times 1024 or 3072 bytes – 3072 numbers between 0 and 255. In the "for" loop in Listing 85, we go through each byte in the file and display its numerical value on the screen. If we tried to print the contents of "image.dat" in text format, we would just see nonsensical data and weird characters on the screen, as the file is not meant to be processed as plain text. By displaying the numbers in human readable format, we can see what each byte contains, even if the values don't mean much to us right now.

For large files, you may not want to read them all in one lump – especially when you're trying to save memory. It's possible to load individual bytes from the file on an as-needed basis, although it's a little more involved:

```
Command Prompt                    —    □    ×
C:\Users\mike\Desktop\codingmanual>python
listing85.py
66 77 138 16 0 0 0 0 0 138 0 0 0 124 0 0
 0 32 0 0 0 32 0 0 0 1 0 32 0 3 0 0 0 0 16
 0 0 19 11 0 0 19 11 0 0 0 0 0 0 0 0 0 0
 0 0 255 0 0 255 0 0 255 0 0 255 0 0 0 66
71 82 115 0 0 0 0 0 0 0 0 0 0 0 0 0 0 0
0 0 0 0 0 0 0 0 0 0 0 0 0 0 0 0 0 0 0
0 0 0 0 0 0 0 0 0 0 2 0 0 0 0 0 0 0 0
0 0 0 0 0 0 0 0 0 0 0 0 0 0 0 0 0 0 0
0 0 0 0 0 0 0 0 0 0 0 0 0 0 0 0 0 0 0
0 0 0 0 51 0 234 234 227 0 237 234 253 0 2
44 234 255 0 251 234 255 0 254 234 255 0 2
54 234 255 0 254 234 255 0 254 234 255 0 2
```

We can read binary data and show the numbers contained within each byte of the data – like we do in Listing 85.

LISTING 86:

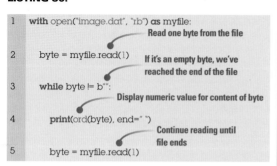

```
1    with open("image.dat", "rb") as myfile:
                          Read one byte from the file
2        byte = myfile.read(1)
                          If it's an empty byte, we've
                          reached the end of the file
3        while byte != b"":
                          Display numeric value for content of byte
4            print(ord(byte), end=" ")
                          Continue reading until
                          file ends
5            byte = myfile.read(1)
```

On line 2 here, the "read" operation takes a byte from the file and returns a special data type called a byte object. We need to use specific formatting to work with this, so on line 3 we check if it's empty, using the "b" before the quotation marks to make it clear we're working with a byte. If the byte is empty, that means we've reached the end of the file – so the loop stops. Otherwise, on lines 4 and 5 we print the value contained in the byte in human-readable format using "ord", get another byte from the file and continue with the loop.

We're getting into quite advanced territory here, and ultimately your uses for binary data will depend entirely on the specific programs you end up writing. Explaining how to parse various image, sound and video formats is way beyond the scope of this book (just the specifications alone for many of those are even bigger than this guide!) but now you have the fundamentals and can investigate the structure of specific file formats at a later time.

 Getting file names from the command line

Up until this point, we've been using file names that are hard-coded into the program. In many cases you'll want the user to provide a file name, however, and usually at the start, when they run the program. For instance, if the user types "python test.py data.txt", then he/she is supplying "data.txt" as an extra parameter, telling the program to handle it. So how do we get this information in our Python code?

Well, we have to ask the operating system (OS) for a bit of help. The OS can tell freshly started Python programs what extra parameters were given at the command line. To do this, we tell Python that we need to access some system ("sys") information, getting all command-line parameters (aka "arguments") into a list that we can use. That's what we do here:

LISTING 87:

```
1    import sys
2
3    if len(sys.argv) == 1:
4        print("No filename specified!")
5        sys.exit(1)
6
7    try:
8        file_data = open(sys.argv[1], "r").read()
9        print(file_data)
10
11   except OSError as err:
12       print("File couldn't be opened:")
13       print(err)
```

On line 1, we import an add-on chunk of Python functionality into our program, which gives us access to some system information and services. (We cover exactly what "import" does later in the book, so stay tuned!) Once we've done this, "sys.argv" contains a list of arguments that the user entered at the command line when running the program.

There's something very important to note here: the first item in the list, "sys.argv[0]", is the name of the program itself – so "test.py" or "listing87.py" or whatever you called it. This means that the first actual file name that the user entered after "python test.py" ends up in "sys.argv[1]". If the user added more arguments when running the program, those will be in "sys.argv[2]", "sys.argv[3]" and so on.

So to find out if the user provided an extra file name parameter, we do a check on line 3: if there is only one item in the "sys.argv" list, that's just the name of the Python program itself, which means the user didn't specify a file name. In this case we print a message and exit back out to the operating system (with an error code of 1, in case the operating system needs it – we often use 1 for errors and 0 if the program exits after running successfully).

If there is more than one item in the 'sys.argv' list, however, then it means the user added a file name; this will be in 'sys.argv[1]' as mentioned. So from line 7 onwards we try to open and read this file, bailing out with an error if the file can't be read or doesn't exist.

SAVING YOUR RESULTS
Searching through files

If you need to find a specific piece of information inside a file, Python offers a few ways to do this. First, create a plain text file called "data.txt" with the following four lines of content:

```
Fly me to the moon
Let me play among the stars
Let me see what spring is like
On a-Jupiter and Mars
```

Let's say your program needs to find out where the word "spring" can be found in this file. If we go through it line by line, we can use the following method:

LISTING 88:

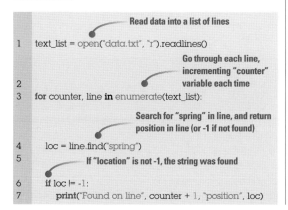

```
                    Read data into a list of lines
1    text_list = open("data.txt", "r").readlines()
                         Go through each line,
                         incrementing "counter"
2                        variable each time
3    for counter, line in enumerate(text_list):
                    Search for "spring" in line, and return
                    position in line (or -1 if not found)
4        loc = line.find("spring")
5            If "location" is not -1, the string was found
6        if loc != -1:
7            print("Found on line", counter + 1, "position", loc)
```

We looked at "enumerate" back in Listing 59, and it lets us work through a list while also keeping track of which item we're on. So on the first iteration of this loop, "counter" contains 0 – referring to "text_list[0]", the first line in the file. On the next iteration, "counter" becomes 1, and so on. And with each iteration of the loop, the text content is placed in our "line" string variable.

Line 4 of the code does the magic here: it searches for the text "spring" in the "line" string variable, and returns its position if it's found (i.e. after how many characters). If "spring" can't be found, "loc" gets the value -1. So we can

 Tip

Want to ignore case in your searches? This is possible too: the best approach is to search for a lowercase string in a lowercase version of the line data. In this way, everything is lowercase so all matches will be found. To do this, modify "line.find" on line 4 of Listing 88 to be "line.lower().find" – which generates a lowercase version of the text in "line". (Note that it doesn't actually change the contents of "line" permanently – just for this comparison.) Now use a lowercase string inside the brackets afterwards, and you can find data regardless of case.

check for this on line 6, and then print the position on line 7 if "spring" was found.

Note that we add 1 to our "counter" variable in this case, because even though Python starts counting items in a list from zero as we know, we humans tend to count lines of text starting from 1. So try running this code, changing what to search for on line 4, and see the results.

Finding and changing your position

Let's go back to binary files for a moment – and specifically, loading them one byte at a time, like we did in Listing 86. As we work our way through the file, Python keeps track of exactly which byte we're reading, i.e. our position in the file. We can get Python to "tell" us this information, and indeed jump to a different position in the file if we want to.

In the following example, we work with the "image.dat" file again. We ask the user to enter a number (between 0 and 255), and our program will show which bytes in the file contain that number – in other words, where that number appears in the file. In addition, we ask the user to enter an "offset", which is the position from which we start searching. So if the file is 100KB in size, or around 100,000 bytes, if we enter 50,000 for the offset, Python will only start searching after that point (the second half of the file). Let's see how this works:

LISTING 89:

```
1   num = int(input("Enter a number to find in ↵
    image.dat: "))
2   offset = int(input("Enter an offset to search from: "))
3
4   with open("image.dat", "rb") as myfile:
            Jump to specified position in the file
5       myfile.seek(offset)
6                           Get byte value from current
                            position, and increment position
                            by one byte
7       byte = myfile.read(1)
8       while byte != b"":
                    Does the byte contain the value we're
                    searching for?
9           if ord(byte) == num:
            Returns current byte position in the file
10              print(num, "found at position", myfile.tell() - 1)
11          byte = myfile.read(1)
```

There's a lot of functionality packed into a small chunk of code here, so let's go through it. First off we get two integer numeric values – a number to search for, and the

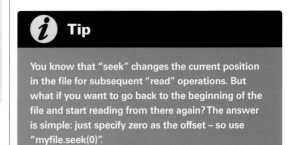

```
Command Prompt                          —  □  ×

C:\Users\mike\Desktop\codingmanual>python
listing90.py
Enter a number to find in image.dat: 154
154 found at position 298
154 found at position 358
154 found at position 542
154 found at position 626
154 found at position 790
154 found at position 890
154 found at position 1166
154 found at position 1282
154 found at position 3086
154 found at position 3202
154 found at position 3478
```

Using the code in Listing 89, we can search for specific bytes within a file, and show the position in the file data at which they occur.

offset in the file where the search should begin – from the user. Next, we open "image.dat" in read-only binary mode, and then on line 5, we "seek" or jump to the position that the user specified. When you first test this program, use 0 (zero) for the offset, and then try changing it to see the difference it makes.

On line 7 we read a byte from the current offset in the file and store it in our "byte" variable, in preparation for the following loop. Note that every time we use "read", Python updates its own internal position counter for the file. When we want to know this position, we ask Python to "tell" us, as you can see on line 10. Because "read" increments the position, by the time we use "tell" on line 10 its position is now after where the number was found. So we subtract 1 from the result to get the true location where the number was found.

Try searching for any number between 0 and 255, and this program will show you exactly which bytes contain those numbers. Then try changing the offset to remove results from earlier bytes.

ⓘ Tip

You know that "seek" changes the current position in the file for subsequent "read" operations. But what if you want to go back to the beginning of the file and start reading from there again? The answer is simple: just specify zero as the offset – so use "myfile.seek(0)".

Let's finish off this subsection with a quite advanced (but potentially useful) technique to add to your Python skill set. In Listing 89 we search for bytes – so numbers between 0 and 255 – but many programs deal with much larger numbers. Given that all files are made up of bytes, how do they express numbers larger than 255? The answer is this: they work with multiple bytes at a time. One byte may contain, say, 24, while the following byte contains 183. Put them together and you get a much larger number. (Note that the larger number isn't merely the sum of the bytes – it's more complicated than that. Here we'll just focus on searching.)

Two bytes together can contain numbers between 0 and 65535. So if we want to modify Listing 89 to handle dual-byte numbers (often referred to as "words"), we need to make some changes. Firstly, we need to read two bytes at a time instead of one; also, we need to tell Python how to interpret those two bytes when they're lumped together as a single number:

LISTING 90:

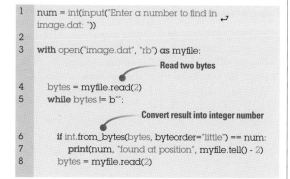

```
1   num = int(input("Enter a number to find in ↵
    image.dat: "))
2
3   with open("image.dat", "rb") as myfile:
                              Read two bytes
4       bytes = myfile.read(2)
5       while bytes != b"":
                              Convert result into integer number
6           if int.from_bytes(bytes, byteorder="little") == num:
7               print(num, "found at position", myfile.tell() - 2)
8           bytes = myfile.read(2)
```

In order to keep this listing simple, we've removed the offset bits of code that we used in Listing 89. On line 4 we read two bytes instead of one, and store them in our "bytes" variable. Then, on line 6, we ask Python to create an integer representation of those two bytes, in order to compare with our "num" variable.

Now, the method used for combining two (or more) bytes into a single number varies by CPU architecture. This is a whole other topic (search for "endianness" on the web if you're interested, but it can get rather complicated!), so all we need to do is set the byte order to be "little" when generating the integer from the bytes – that's the norm for 32-bit and 64-bit PCs and Macs, and most Raspberry Pi setups.

Finally, we display the position on line 7. Remember that at this point, "tell" returns the position after the number

we're searching for, because "read(2)" moved the position on by two bytes after returning its data, so we need to subtract 2 here to get the original position where the number was found.

SAVING YOUR RESULTS
Handling Python data

Back in Listing 84 we looked at loading structured data in comma-separated value (CSV) format. You can use this for your programs when you need to process text and numbers, but chopping up your data and organizing it into the right format can be a bit of a headache. What if you just want to quickly save some Python data to disk, and read it later? Fortunately, there's an elegant way to do this – and it's called "pickling".

Yes, the name is odd, but ignore that: pickling is the process of converting Python data objects (such as lists or dictionaries) into a compact binary form that can be stored in a file, and read back quickly. It has some drawbacks when compared to plain text files – in that you can't simply edit pickled Python data in your usual text editor – but it's very simple to use and doesn't require any complicated parsing techniques. Here's how it works:

LISTING 91:

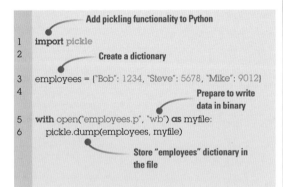

```
          Add pickling functionality to Python
1   import pickle
2            Create a dictionary
3   employees = {"Bob": 1234, "Steve": 5678, "Mike": 9012}
4                        Prepare to write
                         data in binary
5   with open("employees.p", "wb") as myfile:
6       pickle.dump(employees, myfile)
                        Store "employees" dictionary in
                        the file
```

As mentioned before, we'll cover "import" a bit later in the book – all we need to know here is that we add the ability to pickle data to our Python programs. So we create a dictionary, then open (or create if it doesn't exist) an "employees.p" file for writing to in binary mode ("wb"). You can use any file name you like here; we recommend adding the ".p" extension for consistency, so you always know that ".p" files contain pickled data.

Try running this program – it won't display anything, of course, but you'll end up with that "employees.p" file alongside your code. Now have a look inside that file, with "less employees.p" on macOS or Linux, or rename the extension to ".txt" on Windows and try to open it

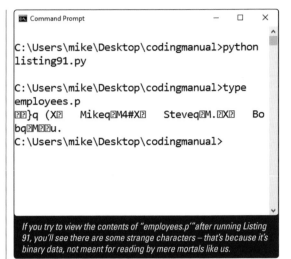

If you try to view the contents of "employees.p" after running Listing 91, you'll see there are some strange characters – that's because it's binary data, not meant for reading by mere mortals like us.

in Notepad. What do you see? Just mostly random gobbledygook, with perhaps a few bits of human-readable data like the names from the dictionary. This format is optimized for Python, even if it doesn't make sense to our eyes.

We've seen that the pickle "dump" routine is used for saving data – but what about loading? Let's get the dictionary back from the "employees.p" file that we just created:

LISTING 92:

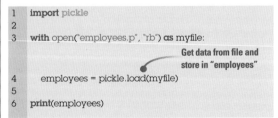

```
1   import pickle
2
3   with open("employees.p", "rb") as myfile:
                        Get data from file and
                        store in "employees"
4       employees = pickle.load(myfile)
5
6   print(employees)
```

This time, we open the file for reading in binary mode (hence "rb" on line 3) and then use pickle's "load" routine to extract the data and place it into "employees". From here onwards, "employees" is a dictionary, which we can examine and manipulate as usual – and, as mentioned, pickling can be used with lists as well.

The JSON alternative

If you've been keeping an eye on the web development scene in recent years, you've probably heard about JSON, also known as "JavaScript Object Notation". This is a plain text format for storing data, and has become hugely popular amongst web developers – largely because JavaScript is booming, both in the web browser and on web servers as well. JSON lets you store data in a way that's easy to process in JavaScript, and Python includes a module to handle it.

In fact, it's almost the same as pickling. Here's how to save a dictionary:

LISTING 93:

```
1  import json
2
3  employees = {"Bob": 1234, "Steve": 5678, "Mike": 9012}
4                                    Write data in
                                     plain text mode
5  with open("employees.json", "w") as myfile:
6     json.dump(employees, myfile)
```

The key differences between this code and Listing 91 are that we import "json" functionality into our program, and when we open the file for writing, we just use "w" for plain text – there's no "b" because we're not writing binary data. JSON is plain text and human readable (although complicated data can be difficult to work through manually), and if you have a peek inside "employees.json" after running this program, you may be surprised.

Tip

In Listing 93 we show how to save or "dump" a JSON representation of a Python object into a file. But what if you just want to display the JSON version on the screen, perhaps for debugging purposes? For this, use "json.dumps", with the extra "s" referring to a string – so in other words, generate a string containing the JSON data. If you add "print(json.dumps(employees))" to Listing 93, for instance, you'll see this in action. And if you have a lot of data and want to make it easier to read, you can add indentation like so: "print(json.dumps(employees, indent=4))", which adds indentation in multiples of four spaces.

It looks just like the dictionary definition on line 3! (Well, the order of the items may be slightly different.) Python's lists and dictionaries and JSON have a lot in common in terms of formatting, but there are some subtle differences so it's important to always convert to the right format and not just assume you can read data because things look similar.

To load JSON data, use the same process as in Listing 92, changing "pickle" to "json" accordingly, and opening the file in text-read mode ("r"). But let's also look at an example of reading more complicated JSON data, where items have multiple sub-items.

Here's a JSON listing for an online shop catalogue, containing two items – both of them are video game consoles. The item first has an identifier or "id" of 1, is called a SNES (Super Nintendo, if you remember those!) and has a price of 199. This item also contains a sublist of bundled "games" – namely "Mario" and "Zelda".

Meanwhile, the second item has an "id" of 2, and is a Sega Mega Drive with a price and bundled games.

```
[
    {
        "id": 1,
        "name": "SNES",
        "price": 199,
        "games": [
            "Mario",
            "Zelda"
        ]
    },
    {
        "id": 2,
        "name": "Mega Drive",
        "price": 149,
        "games": [
            "Sonic",
            "Columns"
        ]
    }
]
```

Note the indentations shown here: they are not required, but they do help to show the structure of the data.

Because this data is a list of items, we open with square brackets. Each item is like a Python dictionary, so they open and close with curly brackets – and we separate the items with a comma, as you can see at the halfway point. For the "games" dictionary entry in each item, we have a list, hence the square brackets. In general, it's very much like the Python data structures we've already worked with, so hopefully you can understand it without too much head-scratching.

Here's a program that reads this "data.json" file, returning the price of the first item in the data (bearing in mind that we count from zero with items, so the first item is the SNES):

LISTING 94:

```
1   import json
2
3   with open("data.json", "r") as myfile:
4       mydata = json.load(myfile)
5
6   print(mydata[0]["price"])
```

Get value for "price" dictionary key from item zero

Line 6 does all the magic here: we use multiple sets of square brackets to narrow down our data. The first tells Python to look at the first item (item zero) in the data, and the second tells it to get the value for "price" key in that item. But let's try a more practical example – how about a program that asks the user to enter an ID, and then prints the details for the item accordingly?

LISTING 95:

```
1   import json
2
3   with open("data.json", "r") as myfile:
4       mydata = json.load(myfile)
5
6   id_to_find = int(input("Enter an item ID: "))
7
8   result = [myitem for myitem in mydata if myitem
    ["id"] == id_to_find]
9
10  if len(result) > 0:
11      print("Name:", result[0]["name"])
12      print("Price:", result[0]["price"])
13      print("Games:", end=" ")
14
15      for games in result[0]["games"]:
16          print(games, end=" ")
17
18      print("")
19  else:
20      print("Not found!")
```

Return value to store in "result"

Go through all items in "mydata" list

Value in "myitem" is returned if this is found

Is the list of results not empty? If so do the following...

"result" is a list containing one item, a dictionary

```
Command Prompt                          —    □    ×

C:\Users\mike\Desktop\codingmanual>python
listing95.py
Enter an item ID: 1
Name: SNES
Price: 199
Games: Mario Zelda

C:\Users\mike\Desktop\codingmanual>python
listing95.py
Enter an item ID: 123
Not found!

C:\Users\mike\Desktop\codingmanual>
```

Here's what happens when we run Listing 95 and search for an item, having converted the JSON data into a list of dictionaries.

Tip

While JSON has become hugely popular in recent years, many apps and services are still using trusty old XML, the Extensible Markup Language. XML looks and works a lot like HTML, but it can be used to store many types of data in a structured and verifiable format. One of the simplest ways to use XML in your Python programs is via the Untangle module, which is described at **http://docs.python-guide.org/en/latest/scenarios/xml/**. This converts XML into a Python data object, which you can then use to access the nodes and attributes.

Wow – that's quite an intricate program, but it teaches us a lot about searching and processing more complex structured data. The most important thing to consider here is that "data.json" contains a single list, denoted by the square brackets, which in turn contains two dictionaries: one for the SNES, and one for the Mega Drive.

So after we get an ID from the user, we perform the searching magic on line 8. This is a new technique for us, but it's called "list comprehension" and lets us generate one list out of another list. We know that our "mydata" list loaded from the file contains two dictionaries – so line 8 generates a new list containing only the dictionary where their "id" key value matches the number we got from the user.

But how does this work? Well, we want our list containing matching dictionary entries to be stored in "result", so we put that at the start of the line. Then we open a list with square brackets, but instead of having a sequence of items as usual, we perform a "for" loop inside the list! The "for myitem in mydata" part goes through each item (each dictionary) in the data, storing the contents in "myitem". The "if" part checks the "id" key in "mydata" each time, to see if it matches the "id_to_find" number. If there's a match, we return "myitem" back to "result" – that's what the first "myitem" in this line does.

These list comprehensions can be quite difficult to understand at first sight, but it helps to break them up into separate chunks: there's the "myitem" at the start, which is the data returned back to "result". There's the "for myitem in mydata" loop, and the "if myitem…" comparison. So we have three things going on in a single line – all packed together.

Finally, we print the appropriate dictionary values based on their keys. Because "result" is a list containing a single dictionary, we need to use "result[0]" to refer to that dictionary inside the list. As always, the best way to really feel at home with the code is to play around with it – try changing data in the JSON file, adding new items, and searching for other values (such as price). With this knowledge, you can already start to build quite advanced data manipulation tools.

? CHALLENGE YOURSELF

1. What character sequence is used to refer to a newline character in Python?
2. What code do you use when opening a file to write to it in binary mode?
3. When reading binary bytes from a file, what command do you use to switch to a specific place in the file?
4. When two bytes are combined together into a word, what is the range of values they can contain?
5. If a user has entered a file name parameter when running our program, how do we access this in our code?

07.

Do more with modules

In this section

What is a module?   88
More goodies from "sys"

Bundled with Python   90
"os" module
"time" module
"math" and "random" modules
"socket" module

Handy extra modules   95
Image manipulation with Pillow
Writing games with Pygame
Graphical (GUI) applications with Tkinter

Challenge yourself   101

At this stage your Python knowledge is becoming quite advanced – in fact, you already know most of the core features of the language. You can perform mathematical operations on data, take input from the user, set up loops and conditions, build your own functions, read and save files, work with lists and dictionaries, and a lot more.

All this is possible with a standard "out of the box" Python installation, but the language is capable of so much more. In order to keep memory requirements low and performance high, Python doesn't roll-in extra functionality unless you explicitly request it. The core language is sleek and lean, which means it can be used on very modest hardware. Indeed, Python can often be found doing the grunt work in embedded devices. Maybe that shiny new internet-enabled fridge you've been eyeing up uses Python scripts to order groceries.

DO MORE WITH MODULES
What is a module?

Put simply, a module is a chunk of Python code that's kept in a separate file. When you want to use the functions and data contained within that file, you "import" it into your own Python code. We've done this already a couple of times in the last section – like when we used "import sys" to access system services, and "import json" so that we can call functions for processing JSON data. Those "sys" and "json" modules are included in a standard Python installation, so they're ready to use whenever we need them.

You may be asking: why do we programmers have to "import" these modules manually at the beginning of our code? Can't Python do all the hard work itself? Well, as mentioned, Python tries to be memory-friendly by default. It can't guess in advance what features you may need in your particular program, and if it loaded all of the modules included every time it ran a program, it would take up a lot more memory. So Python's approach is to offer the basics, and only roll-in extra features when the code explicitly requests them.

Let's look at a module in a bit more detail, and namely "sys", which we used in Listing 87. There, the "sys" module provided us with two useful things: the command-line parameters (aka "arguments"), along with a function called "exit" for terminating a program with an error or success code that's then handed back to the operating system. Note that when we use "import sys", we then have to specify "sys" whenever we use its features, like "sys. argv" or "sys.exit". There's another approach for importing modules, like so:

Tip

The modules supplied with a Python installation are very well documented, at least for reference – but the documentation isn't so great when you're learning on your own. (That's what this book is for!) But for future reference, if you need a list of data and functions provided by a module, you can get them at **https://docs.python.org**. For example, the documentation for "sys" is at **https://docs.python.org/3/library/sys.html** – it's very technical in places but helps if you need to understand exactly what parameters a function takes or returns.

LISTING 96:

```
     Import specific features by name
1    from sys import argv, exit
2
3    if len(argv) == 1:
4        print("No filename specified!")
5        exit(1)
```

This does the same job as the first five lines of Listing 87, but uses "from" in the first line to very explicitly select the features that we want: "argv" and "exit". We can then use those without having to prepend them with "sys.". This is useful in some cases, but for consistency we will use the "import sys" approach in this section, to make it clear which module offers which features.

More goodies from "sys"

The "sys" module provides a few other handy extras that we can use in our programs. If you want to determine which operating system is being used to run your code, you can use "sys.platform" for this – it contains a string with "win32" for Windows (even if it's a 64-bit version of Windows), "linux" for Linux, and "darwin" for macOS. (Darwin was the name Apple gave to the open-source core of macOS back in 2000.)

Then there's "sys.version_info", which is a tuple containing: the major version number, minor version number, micro (or revision) version number, and the release level. If you're running Python 3.5.2, for instance, the major version is 3, minor is 5, and micro is 2. Generally speaking, when the Python developers make major changes to the language, they bump up the major number;

smaller changes and new features get a minor version increment. Micro releases are just for bug fixes and security patches.

The release level is a string containing "alpha", "beta", "candidate" or "final". The first three of these indicate versions of Python that are still being worked on by the developers – so if you want to ensure that your programs are only being run on stable, officially released versions of Python, you can perform a check like in the last two lines of this code:

LISTING 97:

```
1    import sys
2
3    print("Running on:", sys.platform)
4
5    print("Python version: ", end="")
          Separate the version numbers with dots
6    print(sys.version_info[0], sys.version_info[1], sep=".")
7
8    if sys.version_info[3] != "final":
9        print("Error: please use a released version of
         Python!")
10       sys.exit(1)
```

Here we print the OS we're running on, along with the major and minor Python version numbers, and then check the fourth element in the tuple (element number 3, counting from zero) to be sure that it says "final" – if not, we exit out. As we'll see in a moment, you can use these valuable bits of data from "sys" to perform different things depending on the operating system being used.

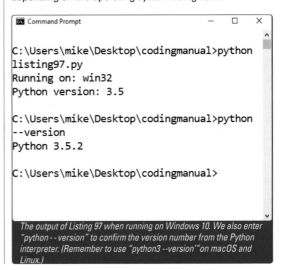

The output of Listing 97 when running on Windows 10. We also enter "python --version" to confirm the version number from the Python interpreter. (Remember to use "python3 --version" on macOS and Linux.)

DO MORE WITH MODULES
Bundled with Python

The "sys" module we've just looked at is merely one of many modules that are provided in a regular Python installation. There are plenty of others to explore as well, so in this subsection we'll look at some of the most useful ones and show you how to work with them.

"os" module

As you might have gathered from the name, this lets your Python programs interface with the operating system (OS). One especially handy routine that it includes is "os. system", which lets you execute a command – just like from the regular command line. For instance, let's say we want to clear the screen at the start of our program. Python provides no specific way to do this, as it's more of an operating system-specific job, so let's get the OS to do it instead.

But then we have a bit of a problem: different OSes use different commands to clear the screen. At the Windows command prompt we use "cls", whereas in macOS and Linux the command is "clear". There's a solution, though! We can use "sys.platform" to see which OS we're running on, and then execute the appropriate command:

LISTING 98:

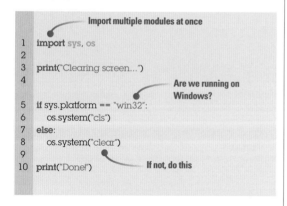

Import multiple modules at once

```
1   import sys, os
2
3   print("Clearing screen...")
4
5   if sys.platform == "win32":
6       os.system("cls")
7   else:
8       os.system("clear")
9
10  print("Done!")
```

Are we running on Windows?

If not, do this

Notice here on line 1 how we import multiple modules at the same time, by separating them with a comma. On line 5 we check to see if our Python code is being executed on Windows; if not, then it will probably be macOS or Linux, both of which use the "clear"

command. (Python runs on other operating systems such as Amiga OS, but the vast majority of users run Windows, macOS or Linux.)

Here's another useful routine from the "os" module: getting the size of the window in which the Python program is being executed. If your program does a lot of work on the screen, you may want to ensure that the command line window is big enough at the start, so that your output doesn't get messed up. The "os.get_terminal_ size" function returns a tuple of two numbers: the width of the screen in characters (i.e. how many columns of characters), and the height in lines.

LISTING 99:

```
1   import os
2
3   width, height = os.get_terminal_size()
4
5   print("Window width:", width)
6   print("Window height:", height)
```

For a full list of "os" functions, including routines for managing files, see the Python documentation at **https://docs.python.org/3/library/os.html**.

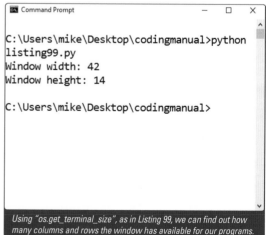

```
Command Prompt                          —   □   ×

C:\Users\mike\Desktop\codingmanual>python
listing99.py
Window width: 42
Window height: 14

C:\Users\mike\Desktop\codingmanual>
```

Using "os.get_terminal_size", as in Listing 99, we can find out how many columns and rows the window has available for our programs.

"time" module

Want to make your program pause for a certain number of seconds? Import the "time" module and use its "sleep" routine. You can even specify floating point numbers (e.g. 0.5 or 0.2) to pause for durations shorter than a second. Here it is in action:

LISTING 100:

```
1   import time
2
3   print("Counting to 10 seconds...")
4
5   for x in range(1, 11):
                        Pause execution for specified
                        number of seconds
6       time.sleep(1)
7       print(x)
```

To get the current time and date in your Python code, there are a few approaches. The simplest is to use the "time" module's "strftime" (string formatted time) routine to generate a customized text string with the details you need. Here's how to get the time in 24-hour clock "hours:minutes" format:

LISTING 101:

```
1   import time
2
3   mytime = time.strftime("%H:%M")
4
5   print(mytime)
```

You're probably asking: what's with the odd formatting inside the string parameter that we send to "strftime" – what do those percentage signs do? They tell "strftime" to replace them with relevant data. "%H" here is converted into the current hour, and "%M" is converted into minutes.

Tip

The "strftime" routine is great for generating detailed human-readable strings with plenty of detail, but if you just need a single piece of information in numeric format, you can get that as well. Just convert the results to an integer using "int". For instance, to get a raw number for the current hour of the day, do this: 'hour = int(time.strftime("%H"))'

So if we run this at half-past two in the afternoon, "mytime" will contain a string with "14:30".

There are other symbols you can use to customize your results: "%S" for seconds, "%A" for the day of the week (e.g. "Saturday"), "%B" for the month name (e.g. "March"), "%m" for the month as a number between 1 and 12, "%Y" for the year, and "%Z" for the time zone (e.g. "GMT"). If you need to put an actual "%" character in your string, just use two of them together: "%%".

"math" and "random" modules

The "math" module is equipped with a bunch of trigonometric functions: "math.cos(x)" returns the cosine of x radians (you can use a number or a variable), "math.tan(x)" returns the tangent of x radians, and so forth – see **https://docs.python.org/3/library/math.html** for a full list. In addition, the module provides a set of "constants", which are numbers that don't change, like π (pi).

Here's a program that calculates the area of a circle based on the radius that's inputted by the user. In real math we know that the area is the square of the radius multiplied by π, so in Python we do:

LISTING 102:

```
1   import math
2
3   radius = int(input("Enter circle radius: "))
                                        Power operator
4
5   print("Area is", round((radius ** 2) * math.pi, 2))
        Round down to 2 decimal places
```

You can see here that the "**" power operator on line 5 generates the square of the radius (power of 2), and we round down the results to make them more readable.

Let's now move on to random numbers, which are especially useful if you're programming games. Imagine that you're coding the movement of an enemy spaceship: if you made it follow the same path all the time, players would easily be able to determine where it's going and blast it accordingly. Add some random movement to the mix, however, and the game becomes a lot more difficult (and the enemies look more realistic!).

To get random numbers, we use the aptly named "random" module. Before we use our first number, though, we need to "seed" the random number generator – that is, initialize it. From there, we can use "random.

randint" followed by a range of numbers to generate a number in that range:

LISTING 103:

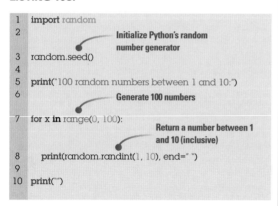

```
1  import random
2              Initialize Python's random
               number generator
3  random.seed()
4
5  print("100 random numbers between 1 and 10:")
6              Generate 100 numbers
7  for x in range(0, 100):
               Return a number between 1
               and 10 (inclusive)
8      print(random.randint(1, 10), end=" ")
9
10 print("")
```

A typical use of random numbers is to perform a specific action when a certain number is generated. Going back to our enemy spaceship example, let's say it's on the top of the screen, moving left and right, and the player is at the bottom (Space Invaders style). We want the enemy to occasionally move down on the screen, but not at regular intervals – we want to surprise the player!

So for every time the enemy moves left and right, there should be a random chance it moves downwards. We can set this chance as 20% of its regular moves, by generating a number between 1 and 5, and only moving down when 1 comes up. This program has a loop simulating 20 moves of the enemy, showing "moving down" 20% of the time (1 in 5) and "staying still" for the rest:

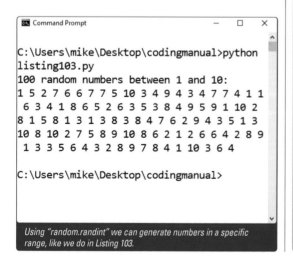

```
C:\Users\mike\Desktop\codingmanual>python
listing103.py
100 random numbers between 1 and 10:
1 5 2 7 6 6 7 7 5 10 3 4 9 4 3 4 7 7 4 1 1
 6 3 4 1 8 6 5 2 6 3 5 3 8 4 9 5 9 1 10 2
8 1 5 8 1 3 1 3 8 3 8 4 7 6 2 9 4 3 5 1 3
10 8 10 2 7 5 8 9 10 8 6 2 1 2 6 6 4 2 8 9
 1 3 3 5 6 4 3 2 8 9 7 8 4 1 10 3 6 4

C:\Users\mike\Desktop\codingmanual>
```

Using "random.randint" we can generate numbers in a specific range, like we do in Listing 103.

LISTING 104:

```
1  import random
2
3  random.seed()
4              Go through 20 moves
5  for x in range(1, 21):          Each move,
6      print("Move", x, end="")    generate random
7                                   number between
                                    1 and 5
8  myrandnum = random.randint(1, 5)
9              Number 1 will be generated around 20% of the time
10 if myrandnum == 1:
11     print(" - moving down")
12 else:
13     print(" - staying still")
```

Run this program a few times, and you'll see that the results are always different (or at least should be, but as with everything random, there's a chance that the same set of results can come up!). On average, the "moving down" message should occur roughly 20% of the time, but it will vary.

You can use random numbers for all sorts of things – choosing elements in a tuple or list, choosing cards from a deck in a poker game, and much more. See **https://docs.python.org/3/library/random.html** for a list of other random-related routines.

 Tip

An alternative to "random.randint" is "random.randrange", which takes three parameters: a starting number, an ending number, and a gap between possible results – so if you wanted to generate an **odd** random number between 1 and 20, you'd use "random.randrange(1, 20, 2)". The 2 at the end here means: after 1, there should be a gap of 2 until the next possible result, which is 3. Then another gap of 2 so the next possible result is 5, and on it goes.

"socket" module

Network programming is an entire topic of its own and warrants a whole book, but we'll show you the essentials here which you can use later with other modules for specific jobs. If you want your Python programs to access another computer on a network – be it a local network in your home or office, or the worldwide internet – then you need to establish a connection to a "socket" on that other computer.

Let's take web browsing as an example. When you fire up your browser and go to a website, your computer establishes a network connection to a socket on the computer that hosts that website. Now your computer and the computer hosting the website (the web server) can talk to each other over the network, with both computers sending and receiving data.

Your web browser kicks off the process by saying to the web server: "Hi there, I'm a web browser. Can you send me your base (/) page data please?" The website's web server processes the request and sends back HTML, CSS and other data. When the user clicks a link in the browser, the process is repeated, but your browser asks for a specific page rather than just the base (/) starting page.

Here's a Python program that does this job. It connects to a network socket on an internet web server, sends and receives data over the socket, and prints the results to the screen:

LISTING 105:

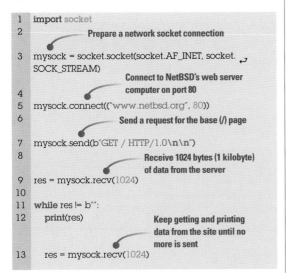

```
1   import socket
2            Prepare a network socket connection
3   mysock = socket.socket(socket.AF_INET, socket.
    SOCK_STREAM)
             Connect to NetBSD's web server
             computer on port 80
4
5   mysock.connect(("www.netbsd.org", 80))
6            Send a request for the base (/) page
7   mysock.send(b"GET / HTTP/1.0\n\n")
             Receive 1024 bytes (1 kilobyte)
             of data from the server
8
9   res = mysock.recv(1024)
10
11  while res != b"":
12      print(res)
             Keep getting and printing
             data from the site until no
             more is sent
13      res = mysock.recv(1024)
```

On line 3 here, we create a new socket connection called "mysock" and provide a couple of parameters; you don't

```
C:\Users\mike\Desktop\codingmanual>python listing105.py
b'HTTP/1.1 200 OK\r\nDate: Fri, 09 Dec 2016 14:06:40 GM
T\r\nServer: Apache/2.4.23 (Unix)\r\nLast-Modified: Thu
, 01 Dec 2016 09:30:00 GMT\r\nETag: "49c0-542957732a79d
"\r\nAccept-Ranges: bytes\r\nContent-Length: 18880\r\nX
-Frame-Options: SAMEORIGIN\r\nX-Xss-Protection: 1; mode
=block\r\nConnection: close\r\nContent-Type: text/html;
 charset=ISO-8859-1\r\n\r\n\t<!DOCTYPE HTML PUBLIC "-//W3
C//DTD HTML 4.01 Transitional//EN"\n\t"http://www.w3.or
g/TR/html4/loose.dtd">\n\n<html>\n  <head>\n    <meta h
ttp-equiv="Content-Type" content="text/html; charset=IS
O-8859-1">\n     <!-- Copyright (c) 1994-2011\n\t The Ne
tBSD Foundation, Inc.  ALL RIGHTS RESERVED. -->\n    <l
ink rev="made" href="mailto:www@NetBSD.org">\n     <link
```

Here's a very rudimentary Python web "browser" (HTML getter), from Listing 105, showing the HTML code that makes up www.netbsd.org. It demonstrates how we can connect to remote systems.

need to concern yourself with what they mean (it gets very complicated very quickly!) but they're all we need for a simple connection to another machine. On line 5, we then attach this socket to a specific computer on the internet – namely the server that hosts the NetBSD website, **www.netbsd.org**. We connect to port 80 on that computer, which is used for sending website data. (Other ports are used for email, messaging and other services.)

Why the NetBSD website in this example? It's a simple web page designed to be read by many different browsers and computers, so it works well with our code. You can try changing it to other websites when you run the program (you don't need the "http://" prefix), but your results will vary. At least with the NetBSD site, we get back some HTML that we can understand.

ℹ️ Tip

In Listing 105, the double brackets '((" and "))' on line 5 may have thrown you a bit. The "mysock. connect" function obviously needs two parameters – the computer to connect to, and the port number – so why can't we just specify them in a single pair of brackets like usual? This is because the "connect" function expects those parameters as a tuple. We know that the values inside a tuple are surrounded by brackets, so the inner brackets there are for the tuple itself. The outer brackets are for sending parameters to the function as usual.

So we're connected over the internet to the computer that hosts the NetBSD website, on port 80. On line 7, we send a request as a sequence of bytes, asking the NetBSD web server to send us the base (/) page using version 1.0 of the HTTP protocol. You can change the "/" page to something else, such as "/docs/", to get back different data. Yes, we are actually creating an extremely rudimentary web browser here!

Once we have sent our request, we need to listen on the socket for data coming back in. That's what we do on line 9: we wait for the web server to send back 1024 bytes of data, receive it into our "res" string variable, and then start a loop. In this loop, we print the data we get, ask for more data, and stop the loop when the web server has nothing more to send (i.e. when the whole page has been sent). Try this out – you'll see lots of HTML data, and if you go to **www.netbsd.org** in your proper web browser, you'll see the nicely formatted version.

So now you know how to connect to another computer over the network, and send and receive data. The exact data you transfer will depend on the network protocol you want to use – and as mentioned, those are topics for stand-alone books. To whet your appetite, though, see **https://en.wikipedia.org/wiki/Lists_of_network_protocols** for a list, and make yourself a nice cup of tea – there's a lot of reading material there.

 ### Creating your own modules

Making your own modules is easy, and highly recommended when you start writing longer and more powerful programs. You'll notice that you end up reusing lots of bits of code between your programs, and while copying and pasting functions is one way to do this, it has its limitations. If you have five programs that all include the same "process_data" function that you created, and then you spot a bug in the function, what can you do? You need to update "process_data" in every program that uses it – which is far from ideal, of course.

It's much better to put the code in a separate module that all of your programs can then access. Then there's only one copy of the code so if you update it in the module, all programs using the module benefit immediately. Modules are really just Python files, so to see how they work, create a file called "mymodule.py" with the following content:

LISTING 106:

```
1   def greet_user(name):
2       print("Hi there", name)
3
4   cool_number = 9000
```

This code doesn't do anything important, but it sets up a function and a variable. If you run this code on its own, nothing will happen – so let's use it as a module. Go back to your "test.py" code and enter this:

LISTING 107:

```
1   import mymodule
2
3   mymodule.greet_user("Bob")
4
5   print(mymodule.cool_number)
```

Pretty simple, isn't it? We import our "mymodule" module, noting that we don't need the ".py" extension, and that the file must be in the same directory as the code we're working on. Then we call the "greet_user" function from that module and display its "cool_number" variable as well.

DO MORE WITH MODULES
Handy extra modules

We've explored some of the useful modules bundled with Python, but there are hundreds of other modules created by other developers, all available on the internet. They cover pretty much everything you could imagine doing in Python, from manipulating images and creating music to making games and developing graphical user interfaces. Even better, you can get most of them with single commands – rather than having to trawl through websites to find download links.

Python's built-in module manager is called "Pip", and lets you download and install add-on third-party modules with minimum effort. All you need to do is enter "pip3 install" followed by the name of the module. Note that many modules are actually collections of modules with other supporting software (such as libraries), and together these are known as "packages". Here we'll look at some of the best modules and packages.

Image manipulation with Pillow

Pillow is based on a module called "PIL", the Python Imaging Library, and can be used to manipulate and perform operations on image files. You can get it by entering "pip3 install pillow" at your command prompt – handily, it's the same command on Windows, macOS and Linux. To see how it works, find a PNG image on the web and save it as "image.png" in the directory alongside your Python code. Then run this:

LISTING 108:

```
1    from PIL import Image
2
3    orig_pic = Image.open("image.png")
4
5    print("Format:", orig_pic.format)
6    print("Width:", orig_pic.size[0])
7    print("Height:", orig_pic.size[1])
```

Here we import the "Image" functions from PIL, and then on line 3 we open the "image.png" file that we downloaded beforehand. After this, "orig_pic" can be used to reference the image data. We call it "orig_pic" for the original picture data, in case we make a copy for changes later. For instance, "orig_pic.format" is a string containing the image format ("PNG", "JPEG" etc.) while

"orig_pic.size" is a tuple containing two numbers for the width and height.

Let's look at a more practical example. In Listing 109, we ask the user for a file name, and then we add an effect to the image (a blur), shrink it down to a thumbnail size, and save the results in JPEG format:

LISTING 109:

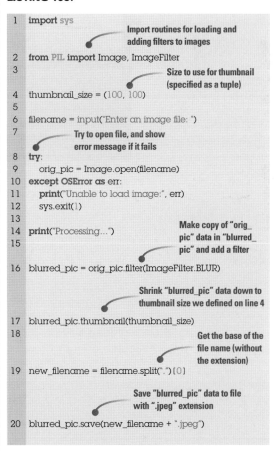

```
1    import sys
                         Import routines for loading and
                         adding filters to images
2    from PIL import Image, ImageFilter
3                        Size to use for thumbnail
                         (specified as a tuple)
4    thumbnail_size = (100, 100)
5
6    filename = input("Enter an image file: ")
7            Try to open file, and show
            error message if it fails
8    try:
9        orig_pic = Image.open(filename)
10   except OSError as err:
11       print("Unable to load image:", err)
12       sys.exit(1)
13
14   print("Processing...")
                         Make copy of "orig_
                         pic" data in "blurred_
                         pic" and add a filter
15
16   blurred_pic = orig_pic.filter(ImageFilter.BLUR)
                         Shrink "blurred_pic" data down to
                         thumbnail size we defined on line 4
17   blurred_pic.thumbnail(thumbnail_size)
18                       Get the base of the
                         file name (without
                         the extension)
19   new_filename = filename.split(".")[0]
                         Save "blurred_pic" data to file
                         with ".jpeg" extension
20   blurred_pic.save(new_filename + ".jpeg")
```

This time we import the "ImageFilter" routines from PIL as well as "Image", get a file name from the user, and try to open it. If the file can't be opened, we use an exception handler to show a message and "sys.exit" to terminate the program.

If the file can be opened, however, then we have its image data in "orig_pic". On line 16, we apply a blur filter to the image data, and store the results in "blurred_pic". Then, on line 17 we shrink down "blurred_pic" according to the dimensions we specified in the tuple on line 4. Note here that the image ratio stays the same: if the image is wider than it is longer, then it will be reduced down to 100 pixels in width, and a smaller amount in height.

Now, we want to save the results in JPEG format, using the original filename with a "jpeg" extension. If we simply added "jpeg" on to the end of the original filename, it would look a bit ugly – like "image.png. jpeg". We just want "image. jpeg", so on line 19 we use "split" on the filename to generate multiple strings, using a period as the separator. If the user entered "image.png" at the start, element zero in the results from "split" will be "image", while item 1 will be the "png" extension. We only need item zero, so we get that into a new file name string.

Lastly, we save the "blurred_pic" image data to a new file, adding ".jpeg" as the extension. Try it out – and, of course, try playing with the parameters! Some of the other effects you can use are EDGE_ENHANCE, EMBOSS, SMOOTH and SHARPEN. You can use Pillow to crop images, perform geometrical transformations,

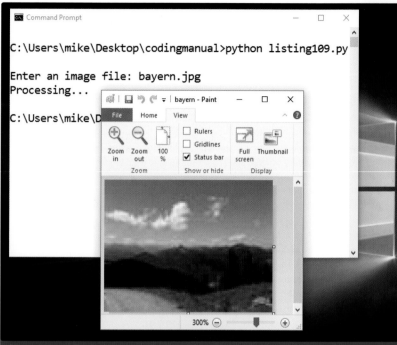

Pillow can be used to add effects to images and generate thumbnails – like we do in Listing 109 (the picture is zoomed in to show the thumbnail's resolution).

manipulate colors and much more, so see the very detailed handbook at **https://pillow.readthedocs.io/ en/latest/handbook/** for all the details.

Writing games with Pygame

We know that many of you reading this book will be interested in video game development. It's fun, it's stimulating, and it can be quite a lucrative career if your games become well-known hits! Modern games are written in a variety of programming languages, but the core concepts are the same regardless of the language you choose. Here we'll focus on 2D games – so using the knowledge we build up here, you can create shoot 'em ups, side-scrolling platformers and other genres. (Oh, and if you're not interested in games at all, it's still well worth reading this subsection, as it introduces a few more Python tricks and techniques.)

There's a fantastic module called Pygame that we can install, which provides many useful routines for handling the screen and keyboard, along with functions for loading images, displaying them on the screen, playing sounds and much more. To install it, enter "pip3 install pygame" – the module will be

Tip

Once you've tried out the modules covered in this section, you may be itching to go further, especially if you're already drawing up plans for your programs. The Python wiki has a good list at **https://wiki. python.org/moin/UsefulModules** – it's organized into category, making relevant modules easy to find.

downloaded from the internet and copied into your Python installation. Then test that it's working like so:

LISTING 110:

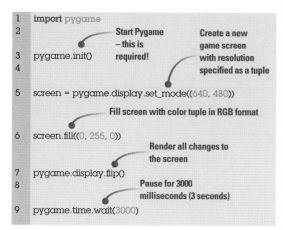

```
1  import pygame
2                    Start Pygame          Create a new
                     – this is            game screen
3  pygame.init()     required!            with resolution
4                                         specified as a tuple

5  screen = pygame.display.set_mode((640, 480))

                     Fill screen with color tuple in RGB format
6  screen.fill((0, 255, 0))
                                  Render all changes to
                                  the screen
7  pygame.display.flip()
                                  Pause for 3000
                                  milliseconds (3 seconds)
9  pygame.time.wait(3000)
```

Every Pygame program has to include a call to "pygame. init" at the start, but we don't need to specify any parameters. On line 5, we create a new screen (a window on our desktop) with the resolution in pixels (dots) specified in a tuple. So here our screen is 640 pixels wide and 480 pixels high. From here onwards, we can use our "screen" object to refer to this screen.

On line 6, we fill this screen with the color green, just to test that the rendering process is working OK. The numbers in the tuple are in RGB (red, green, blue) format, and are byte values from 0 to 255. So 0, 255, 0 means no red, maximum green and no blue – filling the screen with a rich green color.

But we're not quite done yet! For performance reasons, Pygame doesn't actually display all the graphical operations you perform until you call its "flip" routine, so that's what we do on line 7. It's good practice to build up a bunch of screen operations before calling "flip", rather than doing it after every single one. Finally, so that we can see our results, we pause execution for 3000 milliseconds (3 seconds) on the final line. When the program ends, Pygame cleans up and closes the screen.

Now we know how to use Pygame, let's look at some gameplay elements. In this listing we make a ball bounce around the screen – if you want to make the ball image yourself, it should be 32 pixels wide and 32 pixels high, with a transparent background, named "ball.bmp" and placed in the same directory as the code.

LISTING 111:

```
1   import pygame, sys
2
3   pygame.init()
4
5   screen = pygame.display.set_mode((640, 480))
6                                   Load image from file and
                                    store it in our "ball" object
7   ball = pygame.image.load("ball.bmp")

                  Starting positions (X and Y) for the ball
8   ball_x = 10
9   ball_y = 10

                  Amounts to be added to ball position in each loop
10  ball_x_speed = 7
11  ball_y_speed = 7
12
13  while 1:
                            Check for events from the OS, and quit if
                            the window is closed
14      for event in pygame.event.get():
15          if event.type == pygame.QUIT:
16              sys.exit()
17
                            Update ball X and Y positions
18      ball_x += ball_x_speed          If ball goes off
19      ball_y += ball_y_speed          right of screen, set
20                                      negative speed

21      if ball_x > 610: ball_x_speed = -7
22      if ball_y > 450: ball_y_speed = -7

                                  If ball goes off
                                  left of screen, set
23      if ball_x < 0: ball_x_speed = 7    positive speed
24      if ball_y < 0: ball_y_speed = 7
25
26      screen.fill((90, 230, 90))
                            Draw ball at specified X and Y
                            position (in tuple)
27      screen.blit(ball, (ball_x, ball_y))
28
29      pygame.display.flip()
30      pygame.time.wait(10)
```

This is one of our biggest programs so far, and it does a lot! On line 7, we load the "ball.bmp" image and store it in "ball" for future usage. In lines 8 to 9, we set up a few variables: they contain the X (horizontal) and Y (vertical) position of the ball, in pixels on the screen. In Pygame, these start from the top-left, so an X position of 20 and Y position of 300 means this: 20 pixels from the left-hand edge of the screen, and 300 from the top (starting from zero).

Lines 10 and 11 create the starting speed for our ball. Our game runs in a loop, and for each iteration of the loop, we add those numbers onto the ball's X and Y position respectively. This means the X and Y positions go up by 7 each time, which makes the ball move right and down on the screen. The reason we set up these speed variables and not hard-coded numbers in the main code is so we can change them when the ball hits the edge, as we do in a moment.

On line 13 we start an infinite loop, followed by a Pygame "event" check. Essentially, "events" in Python are things that happen due to the user or operating system – such as pressing a key, or closing the window. In lines 14 to 15, we check to see if any events have been generated, and if the event is of type "QUIT", it means the user has closed the window. In this case, we exit out.

Lines 18 and 19 do the work of moving the ball. Each time the loop is executed, we add the contents of the "ball_x_speed" variable onto the ball's X (horizontal) position, and do the same for the Y (vertical) position. Because we set both speed values to be 7, that moves the ball 7 pixels to the right and 7 down each loop. But how do we make the ball bounce when it hits the edges?

That's the magic of lines 21 to 24. These check the ball's horizontal and vertical positions, and say: if the ball is more than 610 pixels across the screen, change the

i Tip

In Listing 111, on lines 21 to 24, you can see that we squeeze our "if" statements and the resulting actions into single lines, rather than using indentation underneath. This is purely a cosmetic change, and it's useful in this book to save some space, but you may want to adopt it in your own programs if you have a lot of "if" statements with short code following them.

number we add to its position each loop to be minus 7. So once "ball_x_speed" becomes -7, that number is added onto "ball_x" each loop, which is the same as subtracting 7 from "ball_x". This makes the ball move backwards, left across the screen!

Why do we check at 610 pixels though, when the screen is 640 pixels wide? Well, remember that the ball itself is 32 pixels wide and high. The "ball_x" and "ball_y" values refer to the top-left of the ball – so if we changed line 21 to check at 640 pixels, the ball would go off the screen before bouncing back. By checking at 610 pixels, the ball is still pretty much entirely visible when it bounces (because 610 + 32 = 642).

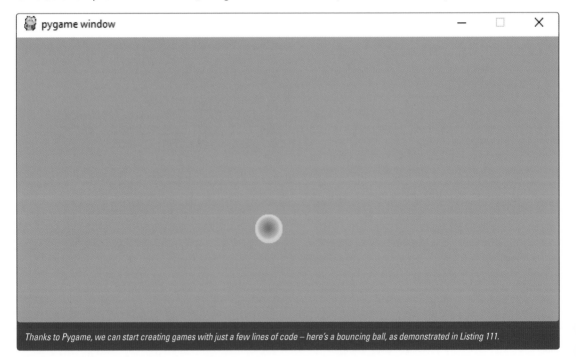

Thanks to Pygame, we can start creating games with just a few lines of code – here's a bouncing ball, as demonstrated in Listing 111.

The same applies to the other checks on lines 22 to 24: if the ball hits an edge of the screen, invert its speed – making the ball bounce around forever. On lines 26 and 27 we fill the screen with a color each loop (to overwrite the previous image data) and then draw the ball at the coordinates specified in the tuple using "blit". Then we "flip" the display to show the new data, and add a pause so that the game doesn't run too quickly. As the loop runs forever, the program only ends when the window is closed.

Graphical (GUI) applications with Tkinter

There are many, many, many (did we say many?) ways to create graphical user interfaces (GUIs) in Python. Annoyingly, most of them are operating system-specific, or require complicated installation procedures – but there's a solution. Python includes its own simple graphical toolkit that doesn't look as shiny as some of the more powerful ones, but lets us create point-and-click apps with relative ease. The toolkit's name is "Tkinter," and here's an example of it in action:

LISTING 112:

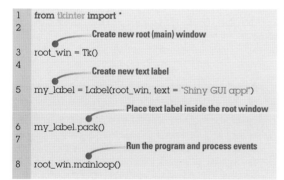

```
1    from tkinter import *
2
                    Create new root (main) window
3    root_win = Tk()
4
                    Create new text label
5    my_label = Label(root_win, text = "Shiny GUI app!")
                    Place text label inside the root window
6    my_label.pack()
7
                    Run the program and process events
8    root_win.mainloop()
```

When creating GUI applications, there are some terms we need to be familiar with. The first thing you'll want to create is the main window, where all the action takes place; this is known as the "root" window, and we create a new one on line 3 here and store it in our "root_win" object.

Then we want to put things inside the window, such as buttons, text entry fields, sliders and other "widgets." On line 5, we add a very simple widget – a text label – by using Tkinter's "Label" routine. This takes two parameters: the first is the window into which it should be placed, and the second is the actual text on the label. On line 6, we use "pack" to actually add the label to the window. Why is it called "pack" though?

Our first graphical user interface program. It doesn't do much at the moment, but we'll soon flesh it out.

If you have a lot of widgets in a window, think about "packing" them all in.

Finally, with our root window all set up and its text label inside, we call the window's "mainloop" routine to start the app. This routine displays the window and waits for events from the operating system, such as mouse clicks and keyboard presses. We don't handle any events ourself in this rudimentary app, but "mainloop" will terminate the program if the user closes the window. Try running this code – the window is very small by default, so resize it to show it in all its glory.

Now, let's move on to a more elaborate and practical example. Back in Listing 102 we wrote a command line

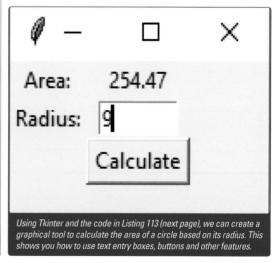

Using Tkinter and the code in Listing 113 (next page), we can create a graphical tool to calculate the area of a circle based on its radius. This shows you how to use text entry boxes, buttons and other features.

program to calculate the area of a circle based on its radius – so how would we implement this in a graphical application? We need some way for the user to input a number, and then to display the results accordingly. This means we need a text entry box (for the radius), a button to click to show the results, and a place in the window where the results will appear. Oh, and we'll need a few text labels as well to show the user what's going on.

LISTING 113:

```
1    import math
2    from tkinter import *
3                  This is run whenever the          Get the contents
                   "Calculate" button is clicked     of "radius" string
4    def calc_area(*args):                           variable (and
                                                      convert to floating
                                                      point number)
5        area_result = (float(radius.get()) ** 2) * math.pi
                   Set contents of "area" string
                   variable (to 2 decimal places)
6        area.set(round(area_result, 2))
7
8    root_win = Tk()      Set window title
9    root_win.title("Area calculator")
                   Set window size
                   (width and height, in pixels)
10   root_win.geometry("200x100")
11                  Create special Tkinter
                    string variable
12   radius = StringVar()
13   radius.set("0")
14   area = StringVar()        Break up long line
15                             into two lines for
                               readability
16   area_label = Label(root_win, text = "Area:") \
17       .grid(column = 1, row = 1)
18                  Specify where label should appear in the window
19   area_value = Label(root_win, textvariable = area) \
20       .grid(column = 2, row = 1)
21         The Tkinter string variable to show
22   radius_label = Label(root_win, text = "Radius:") \
23       .grid(column = 1, row = 2)
24
25   radius_entry = Entry(root_win, width = 7, textvariable = \
26       radius).grid(column = 2, row = 2)
27
28   calc_button = Button(root_win, text="Calculate", \
29       command = calc_area).grid(column = 2, row = 3)
30          Function to run when button is clicked
31   root_win.mainloop()
```

There's a lot happening in this program, so let's step through it bit-by-bit. On lines 1 and 2 we tell Python that we want to use routines from the Math and Tkinter modules, and on lines 4 to 6 we have a function definition for calculating the area of a circle – we'll come back to this later. On line 8 we create a new root window; we then set some extra parameters for this on lines 9 and 10: the window title and its size (width and height, in pixels) respectively.

Line 12 introduces something new. We create a string variable, but instead of doing it the usual Python way by simply placing the original contents of the string in double quotes, we use Tkinter's "StringVar" routine. Why do we do this? If we used normal string variables, whenever they change their values in the Python code, the graphical user interface won't be updated automatically. So we need to use special "StringVar" strings that are deeply integrated with the Tkinter buttons and labels that update on the screen by themselves.

So on lines 12 to 14 we create "radius" and "area" string variables, setting the former to "0". The first will be used to store the radius value that the user enters – while the latter will be calculated on the fly, based on the radius. Next up, on line 16 we create a new text label, like in Listing 112, but with some extra functionality. The backslash (\) character here is used to split up a long line into two lines – so lines 16 and 17 are actually part of the

Tip

Adding '.grid' to our label, text-entry box and button definitions helps us to position items in the window with proper structure, but it has another benefit: we don't need to use extra 'pack' instructions as in Listing 112 to make sure that the widgets appear. So really, in almost every case you'll want to use 'grid' to simultaneously organise the GUI and make your code shorter.

same line. We've split them up for better formatting in the book, but you can remove the backslash so that ".grid..." follows directly on from "area)" on line 16.

Now, what is this ".grid" bit we've tacked on to the label definition? Essentially, it defines where in "root_win" the label should be placed. Think of the root window as made up of rows and columns, like in a spreadsheet: using ".grid" we tell Tkinter that we want this label to be in the first row and first column, i.e. in the top-left.

Line 19 is similar to line 16, but instead of specifying a text string to display, we specify a text variable – our (initially empty) "area" Tkinter string variable created on line 14. We place this in the same row as the previous label, so at the top of the screen, but this time in the second column. The effect is that this text variable appears to the right of the "Area:" label on the left.

Line 22 sets up another label, this time for the radius, on the second row – so it's underneath the two labels above. Then on line 25 we set up an "Entry", which is a text-entry box where the user can type something in. We specify that it should be 7 characters wide, and the results should be stored in the "radius" variable we created on line 12.

Finally, on line 28 we use "Button" for a clickable button with the text "Calculate", and note the third parameter here: "command = calc_area".This tells Tkinter which function should be run when the user clicks the button... and now you can see why we defined our "calc_area" function earlier. Each time the user clicks the "Calculate" button, "calc_area" will be executed.

Let's look inside "calc_area": we don't need the arguments passed to the function so we can ignore the "*args" bit at the start. On line 5, we want to get the content of the "radius" string variable, convert it to a floating point number, and then do the calculation using "math.pi". But watch out! Because "radius" is a special Tkinter string variable, we need to use "radius.get()" to find out what it contains. Similarly, on line 6, we use "area.set()" with the result rounded down to two decimal places in order to update the "area" variable used as a label.

So after all this setting up, line 31 kicks the program into action – try it out and you'll see how the different pieces fit together, how they're laid out in the window, and how the program works. Try changing the row and column positions of the items, the size of the window, and other modifications.

Now you know how to create buttons and link them to functions, you can create some quite advanced GUI apps. For more information on Tkinter, including the various widgets available, start by browsing here: **https://wiki.python.org/moin/TkInter**.

 Other GUI options

As mentioned, Tkinter has the benefit of working "out of the box" on Windows, macOS and Linux, so you don't need to install lots of extras and fiddle around with complicated commands. It's fine for many GUI apps, but if you want more functionality it's worth investigating some alternatives.

One of the most popular cross-platform toolkits (set of widgets for building graphical interfaces) is Qt, and there are two ways to use it in Python: PyQt (**https://wiki.python.org/moin/PyQt**) and PySide (**http://wiki.qt.io/PySide**). Qt is very well maintained and documented, and has a bustling support community on the web, so it's a good choice if you want to make polished applications that run well on multiple operating systems.

Another alternative is wxPython (**www. wxpython.org**), which is based on the wxWidgets toolkit that's commonly used by C++ programmers. Check out the excellent guide at **https://wiki. wxpython.org/Getting%20Started** – you can see that it's quite similar to Tkinter in many respects.

For more GUI toolkit ideas, see **https://wiki. python.org/moin/GuiProgramming**. That page also has a list of Integrated Development Environments (or IDEs), which are like text editors on steroids, helping you write Python code with nifty features like auto-completion and syntax highlighting.

CHALLENGE YOURSELF

1. How can a Python program determine the operating system on which it is running?
2. To make the operating system run "test. exe", what do you do?
3. How can you generate a random number between 20 and 90 (inclusive)?
4. When using Pygame, what must we always do after drawing operations, to make sure the results are visible on the screen?
5. How do you make your own modules?

A class of its own

In this section

What are classes?   **105**

Getters, setters and logic   **107**
Shifting logic into classes

Inheritance   **109**

Using slots   **110**

Challenge yourself   **111**

In the final section of this book, we turn our attention to a feature that is common to many programming languages but which is often misunderstood or overlooked: object-oriented programming (aka OOP). Before we delve into the specifics, however, we need to step back for a moment and consider why it's important. What's the one thing we keep bringing up in this book, which programmers should always strive for?

You may have guessed already: modularity. We've looked at how neatly organized functions, modules and careful attention to variable scope help us to create programs made up of "building blocks." We can reuse functionality in multiple programs, and create general-purpose functions and modules that we can call upon at any time without having to know exactly how they work. OOP plays an equally important role in modularity – so let's explore it.

A CLASS OF ITS OWN
What are classes?

When we write programs using functions, we can include local variables in those functions and make them do different things, depending on the data we send to them (the parameters). That's good, but imagine if we could make individual copies of those functions whenever we needed them, with their own sets of variables and data, all neatly separated from other functions. And on top of that, imagine if we could add sub-functions inside those functions.

In OOP, a "class" is like a function; but whereas normal functions exist and can be used for the entirety of a program's execution, in OOP, we have to create "objects," which contain the data from the class before using them. Sounds a bit weird? Have a look at this:

LISTING 114:

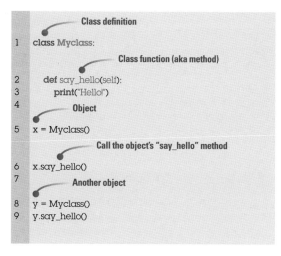

```
1   class Myclass:

2       def say_hello(self):
3           print("Hello!")
4
5   x = Myclass()

6   x.say_hello()
7
8   y = Myclass()
9   y.say_hello()
```

Class definition — line 1
Class function (aka method) — line 2
Object — line 5
Call the object's "say_hello" method — line 6
Another object — line 8

There's some new terminology in here, so let's go through it all. On line 1, we set up a "class definition" – a bit like the function definitions we've worked with before. But a class definition on its own doesn't do anything; it's just a template. (Compare this to a function which we can call straight away from our main code.) Inside this class definition, we create a simple function called "say_hello" – and note that functions inside classes are known as "methods."

As mentioned, this is just a template though; we can't

Tip

You may have noticed that our class names begin with capital letters. This isn't mandatory, but it's good practice and helps you to navigate through larger programs. When you come across a line of code like line 5 in Listing 114, you know straight away from the capital letter that it's creating an instance of a class, and not just running a common-or-garden function.

use this class yet. In order to turn it into something useful, we have to create an "instance" of it – an actual real, working version. This is what we do on line 5. The "Myclass()" bit here looks like a function call, but because it's a class rather than a function, we create an instance of "Myclass" and put the results into "x". And what is "x" now? It's not just a normal variable, but rather an "object" that contains any variables and functions defined by the class.

Line 6 demonstrates this: "x" has its own copy of the "say_hello" function defined by the class, so by using a dot (.) after the object name, we can access its functions (its methods). Then look at what we do on lines 8 and 9: we repeat what we did before, but this time we have a separate object in the form of "y". Both of these objects are instances of the class template we defined at the start, but they exist independently in memory and can be used for different purposes.

Now, because the class definition in Listing 114 always does the same thing and doesn't take any data, it doesn't make much sense to create multiple instances of it – so let's look at classes with variables and data that can be changed. There's a special method we can use in our classes that is automatically executed when a new instance of the class is created: "__init__" (that's "init" with two underscore characters either side).

Let's go back to our employee directory example, and this time create objects for each employee, rather than using normal data structures. When we create each object, we can pass data to the "__init__" method and set up local variables like so:

LISTING 115:

```
1   class Employee:
                    This method is run automatically
                    when objects are created
2       def __init__(self, passed_name, passed_number):
                                    Parameter passed
                                    from the main code
3           self.name = passed_name
                    Instance variable (aka attribute)
4           self.number = passed_number
5
6       def show(self):
7           print("Name:", self.name)
8           print("Number:", self.number)
9
10  first = Employee("Bob", 1234)
11  second = Employee("Steve", 5678)
12
13  first.show()
14  second.show()
```

So when we create new instances of the class on lines 10 and 11 here, the parameters we specify are automatically sucked into the "__init__" method and are available as "passed_name" and "passed_number" variables (but we can call them whatever we want there).

What's going on with all the "self" business in the rest of the class definition, though? This is used to refer back to the object's own copies of variables. If we omitted the "self" here, Python would just think we're creating a temporary variable to be used inside this specific method and nowhere else. But the "self" part tells Python that this is a variable to be stored and shared across all methods in the object. Because of this, our "first" object has its own "name" and "number" variables – aka attributes – while the "second" object has other copies of those variables.

Once we have created an instance of a class, we can modify its attributes using the dot (.) separator, like how we call the functions. For instance, try adding this code snippet to the end of Listing 115:

```
first.name = "Mike"
first.number = 9000
first.show()
```

Here we update the values we set when creating the instance, and show them again.

Class variables – common to all instances

As we've seen in Listing 115, "self" refers to variables owned by a specific instance of a class. But it's also possible to create "class variables" which are shared between **all** instances of a class – i.e. all objects that were instanced from the class. Looking at our employee directory example again, let's say we want to keep track of how many employees have been created. We could do that with a separate variable in the main code, but for the sake of modularity, we want to do this inside the class itself.

We achieve this by declaring the variable inside the class – and before any methods. Here's how it works:

LISTING 116:

```
1   class Employee:
2       employee_count = 0
3
4       def __init__(self, passed_name, passed_number):
5           self.name = passed_name
6           self.number = passed_number
7           Employee.employee_count += 1
8
9       def show(self):
10          print("Name:", self.name)
11          print("Number:", self.number)
12
13  first = Employee("Bob", 1234).show()
14  second = Employee("Steve", 5678).show()
15  third = Employee("Mike", 9000).show()
16
17  print("Number of employees", Employee.
    employee_count)
```

On line 2 here, we create an "employee_count" class variable and set it to zero. This value is shared by all instances of the class. Then, each time an instance is created and "__init__" is executed, that variable is incremented by 1. (Note that we have to prepend it by "Employee." to make it clear that we're referring to the class variable and not just a temporary variable in "__init__".)

On lines 13 to 15, we create new instances of our class – and note the shortcut for creating and then running the "show" method on the same line of code. Finally, on line 17, we display the class "employee_count" variable – and because it's not tied to a specific instance, we prepend it just with "Employee."

A CLASS OF ITS OWN
Getters, setters and logic

Once you've created an instance of a class, and have an object to play with, you can set the attributes inside it in your main code easily – e.g. "first.number = 9000". But sometimes it's useful if the class can perform some checks on values before assigning them to attributes. In this way, the class can ensure that only valid data is being sent to it, making the class (and thereby instances of it) more robust and reliable.

Here's an example of a simple class called Myclass that has one attribute, a numerical variable called "num". Via the "__init__" method we create a "num" attribute with the value passed to it when an instance is created, but then with "@property" and "@num.setter" we create methods that are activated when the main code gets and sets the value of "num" respectively:

LISTING 117:

```
1    class Myclass:
2        def __init__(self, num_passed):
                        Create "num" attribute and set its value
3            self.num = num_passed
4                        Method called whenever the program
                         gets the value of "num"
5        @property
6        def num(self):
7            print("Getting number...")
8            return self.__num
9                        Method called whenever the program
                         sets the value of "num"
10       @num.setter
11       def num(self, num_passed):
12           print("Setting number...")
13           if num_passed > 1000:
14               print("Rounding to 1000")
                        Private variable, used internally
                        in the class
15               self.__num = 1000
16           else:
17               self.__num = num_passed
18
19   x = Myclass(123)
20   print(x.num)
21
22   x.num = 9000
23   print(x.num)
```

Lines 1 to 3 should be familiar by now, and provide each object that is instanced from the class with an attribute called "num". So far, so good, but something special happens here! Every time the "num" attribute gets a new value, including when it is created during "__init__", the method underneath "@num.setter" is called automatically.

This means we can introduce some logic into the method to alter the value if required, before it is applied to "num" – in our case, rounding down if the original passed value is greater than 1000. But why are we setting "self.__num" (with two underscores) here instead of just "self.num" itself? Well, trying to set "num" inside its own setter would result in an infinite loop, with the setter method being called forever! So instead we use a private variable with two underscores, those underscores showing that it should only be used inside the class and not accessed from elsewhere.

The best way to understand how this works is to consider the code flow: when the object is created on line 19, execution jumps to line 2, with "123" as the number being passed. On line 3, when we try to set "num", execution jumps to line 11, again with "123" being passed. From here, we set up a private variable called "__num", which is used to store the real contents of "num", and we perform some logic to round down the number if it's bigger than 1000.

Once the setter has finished, execution continues in the main code block underneath, on line 20. By accessing "x.num", which is the "num" attribute of our "x" object, we trigger the getter, which starts on line 6. This returns the

```
C:\Users\mike\Desktop\codingmanual>python
listing117.py
Setting number...
Getting number...
123
Setting number...
Rounding to 1000
Getting number...
1000

C:\Users\mike\Desktop\codingmanual>
```

The results from Listing 117, showing how the "setter" and "getter" methods are automatically called whenever we read or update a variable.

value of the "__num" private variable we set up before. So any attempts to work with "x.num" in our main code result in the getter or setter being executed, both of which work with the class's private "__num" variable. But from the perspective of the main code, we don't care what happens inside the class – we just know that we can access and set "x.num". The class does all the work internally.

Shifting logic into classes

Another way you can improve modularity and reliability in your programs is to move logic out of your main code and into the classes yourself. Look back at the bouncing ball demo in Listing 111 – how could we make that code more object oriented and do the work of managing the ball movement inside the class itself? Check this out:

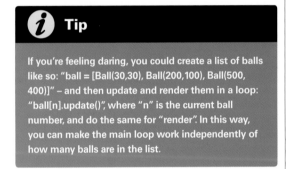

i Tip

If you're feeling daring, you could create a list of balls like so: "ball = [Ball(30,30), Ball(200,100), Ball(500, 400)]" – and then update and render them in a loop: "ball[n].update()", where "n" is the current ball number, and do the same for "render". In this way, you can make the main loop work independently of how many balls are in the list.

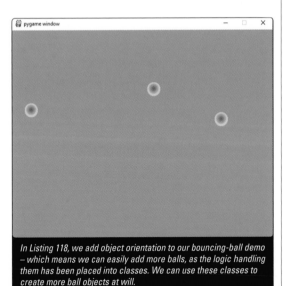

In Listing 118, we add object orientation to our bouncing-ball demo – which means we can easily add more balls, as the logic handling them has been placed into classes. We can use these classes to create more ball objects at will.

LISTING 118:

```
1    import pygame, sys
2
3    class Ball:
                            Set up ball with initial position,
                            speed and image
4      def __init__(self, x, y):
5          self.ball_x = x
6          self.ball_y = y
7          self.ball_x_speed = 7
8          self.ball_y_speed = 7
9          self.ball_pic = pygame.image.load("ball.bmp")
10                          Update ball position and speed
11     def update(self):
12         self.ball_x += self.ball_x_speed
13         self.ball_y += self.ball_y_speed
14
15         if self.ball_x > 610: self.ball_x_speed = -7
16         if self.ball_y > 450: self.ball_y_speed = -7
17         if self.ball_x < 0: self.ball_x_speed = 7
18         if self.ball_y < 0: self.ball_y_speed = 7
19                          Draw ball on the screen
20     def render(self):
21         screen.blit(self.ball_pic, (self.ball_x, self.ball_y))
22
23
24   pygame.init()
25
26   screen = pygame.display.set_mode((640, 480))
27
28   ball1 = Ball(30, 30)
29   ball2 = Ball(200, 100)
30   ball3 = Ball(500, 400)
31
32   while 1:
33      for event in pygame.event.get():
34          if event.type == pygame.QUIT:
35              sys.exit()
36
37      screen.fill((90, 230, 90))
38
39      ball1.update()
40      ball1.render()
41      ball2.update()
42      ball2.render()
43      ball3.update()
44      ball3.render()
45
46      pygame.display.flip()
47      pygame.time.wait(10)
```

This may be longer than the program in Listing 111, but it has a huge benefit, namely: the ball is now an object, rather than being hard-coded into the main code. Indeed, it means we can create and animate more than one ball, and in this enhanced program we do exactly that!

Our "Ball" class has three methods: "__init__" is used to set the initial starting position, which is provided via parameters from the main code. Inside this method we also set up the ball's starting speed, and the image ("ball.bmp") that should be used to display it. So every time we create an instance of "Ball", we get this data set up.

Next, we call each ball's second method – "update" – in each loop of the game. This updates the ball's position and speed accordingly, and because it's done inside the class rather than in the main code, it works on a ball-by-ball basis. Each ball we create has its own attributes and

methods, so all of the balls work independently. Finally, we have a "render" method to show the ball; we could put this in the main code, but it's better to have it in the class in case we want to add more effects or change the rendering process later.

So now, our main code is shorter and more elegant. On lines 28 to 30 we create three balls with their starting positions, before kicking off the main loop. As before, we check to see if the user has closed the window; otherwise we fill the screen and process the three balls by calling their "update" and "render" methods. Because all the balls have different starting positions, they move around independently – try adding more balls and starting positions.

A CLASS OF ITS OWN
Inheritance

The next concept we're going to look at in OOP is called inheritance. This has nothing to do with gaining money or property in a will, but it's a way for classes to build upon other classes, "inheriting" their methods and attributes. Why would you want to do this? Well, consider how you'd handle lots of very similar types of data that have a few crucial differences – and you want to process this data using OOP. You could create separate, distinct classes for every type of data, but there'd be a lot of code repetition and it wouldn't be very efficient.

So a better approach is to define a "base" class that has common elements, and then "subclasses" which inherit characteristics from the base one. Here's a good example of this: imagine you're writing a game or simulation that involves many different types of vehicles, and you want to give each vehicle type its own class. What attributes would be common across them?

All vehicles would have an X and Y position on the screen, along with a speed. All vehicles may also have common methods to move and render them on the screen, like the balls in Listing 118. All of these can go in a "Vehicle" base class – and then we can start to think about subclasses for our specific vehicle types. A digger, for instance, needs all the functionality of the "Vehicle" class but would also have specific methods for only things the digger can do, such as "dig". Similarly, a helicopter class could also need to be based on the "Vehicle" class,

but would need its own "z_pos" (height) variable as it can leave the ground. Take a look at this:

LISTING 119:

```
1   class Vehicle:
2       def __init__(self, x, y):
3           self.x_pos = x
4           self.y_pos = y
5           self.x_speed = 0
6           self.y_speed = 0
7
8       def update(self):
9           print("Moving...")
10          self.x_pos += self.x_speed
11          self.x_pos += self.y_speed
12
13      def render(self):
14          print("Drawing...")
15
16  class Digger(Vehicle):
17      def __init__(self, x, y):
18          Vehicle.__init__(self, x, y)
19
20      def dig(self):
21          print("Digging...")
22
```

Inherit methods and attributes from "Vehicle" class

Initialise the "Vehicle" bits first...

Then add this "dig" method, specific to this "Digger" class

```
23   class Helicopter(Vehicle):
24      def __init__(self, x, y, height):
25         Vehicle.__init__(self, x, y)
26         self.z_pos = height
27                    Attribute specific to this "Helicopter" class

28   car = Vehicle(10, 20)
29   car.update()
30   car.render()
31
32   digger = Digger(50, 90)
33   digger.dig()
34                 Only instances of "Digger" class can call
                   this method
35   chopper = Helicopter(200, 400, 50)
36   chopper.update()
```

Tip

Listing 119 demonstrates how you can make one class inherit from another one, but you can make your classes inherit from multiple classes as well – just place them, separated by commas, inside the brackets during the class definition. Note that this can make your programs very complicated and hard to debug, however, so only do it if you absolutely need it!

To keep the code listing short here and focus on inheritance, we've omitted any game/simulation logic – we've just added a few "print" instructions to show what's going on. The "Vehicle" class created on line 1 is straightforward and follows the principles we've discussed before. It has a few attributes and methods that will be common to all vehicles.

On line 16, though, we do something different: next to the name of the class, we add in brackets the name of the class which we want to inherit. So the "Digger" class now has all the attributes and methods from "Vehicle", without us having to code them all separately. That's a good time-saver! Still, we need to make sure that the "Vehicle's" own "__init__" routine is called – so that's what we do on line

18, passing the values we receive. On line 20, we define a method call "dig" which is specific just to this class. Normal instances of the "Vehicle" base class won't be able to use this method; only instances of "Digger".

The "Helicopter" class on line 23 also inherits from "Vehicle", and runs that class's "__init__" routine, but also adds its own "z_pos" attribute variable, used to track the height of the vehicle. Only objects created from instances of "Helicopter" will be able to use this attribute – not regular vehicles or diggers. On lines 28 to 36 we show how this works: if you try "car.dig()" you'll get an error, and you can see that we need to pass three parameters on line 35 when creating a "Helicopter" object. The final line simply demonstrates how we can still use the "Vehicle" base class's "update" method because "Helicopter" inherited it.

A CLASS OF ITS OWN
Using slots

To wrap up this section, we'll look at a way to have more control over your objects – and specifically, the attributes that they can have. Normally, when you create objects, you can add extra attributes to them during the course of your program, even if they're not in the class definition itself. Here's a program demonstrating this in action:

LISTING 120:

```
1    class Myclass:
2       def __init__(self, passed_number):
3          self.number = passed_number
4
5    x = Myclass(10)
6    print(x.number)
7
8    x.text = "Hello"
9    print(x.text)
10
11   print(x.__dict__)
```

Here we set up a new class definition as usual, which contains a single attribute called "number". When we create an instance of this class on line 5, we set a value of 10 for that attribute. So far, so good – but what happens on line 8? Here we create a new attribute for this instance of the class, a text-string attribute, even though the class definition didn't specify it.

Now, this is fine; for many of your programs, the ability to create new attributes on the fly is a benefit. There are some drawbacks, however: the attributes are stored in a dictionary, which takes time to process and isn't very efficient with RAM. This object-specific dictionary is called "__dict__" (two underscores on each side), and in Listing 120 we show the contents of it: "{'number': 10, 'text': 'Hello'}".

To improve performance and save memory, you can tell Python not to use a dictionary to store instance attributes. Instead, you can specify exactly which attributes are allowed, so that no others can be created. This is achieved using "slots", and it works like so:

LISTING 121:

```
1   class Myclass(object):
2       __slots__ = ["number", "name"]
3       def __init__(self, passed_number):
4           self.number = passed_number
5
6   x = Myclass(10)
7   print(x.number)
8
9   x.name = "Bob"
10  print(x.name)
11
12  x.text = "Hello"
```

There are two main changes here from Listing 120: on line 1, we specify that "Myclass" should inherit from the generic "object" class, and on line 2, we set up our "__slots__" (with the now-familiar double underscores each side), specifying exactly which attributes are allowed in instances of this class. So we say that "number" and "name" are allowed – nothing else.

In the main code starting from line 6, we create those "number" and "name" attributes – but look at what happens on line 12. Here we're trying to create a new instance attribute called "text", but Python doesn't like this; it terminates the program with an error: "AttributeError: 'Myclass' object has no attribute 'text'."

As mentioned, using slots to specify attributes can lead to performance improvements and memory savings. You won't notice it in small and simple programs like in

Listings 120 and 121, but if you're writing a more complex application that creates thousands of objects and needs to process them rapidly, using slots rather than the default dictionary can make a difference.

As an example, here's a blog post from an engineer at a hotel reviews website which uses Python extensively. Just by using slots and adding a single line of code, the engineer managed to save over 9GB (yes, gigabytes!) of RAM across his web servers: **http://tech.oyster.com/save-ram-with-python-slots/.**

CHALLENGE YOURSELF

1. What do we call a function inside a class definition?
2. How can we quickly tell the difference between a function call, and creating an instance of a new class?
3. What is special about the "__init__" method?
4. What is a "setter"?
5. What is a "class variable"?

The end of the book – but the start of your coding career

And with this, we come to the end of the book (or at least, the main sections – don't miss the example programs and resources for further reading). We've explored Python in great detail, and now you have the skills, techniques and knowledge to start writing your own programs. Or if you want to work on an existing Python project, you can now understand and modify other people's code – well, providing that it's well written code, of course!

We hope you have found the book useful, stimulating and fun to work through, and wish you all the best with your new programming hobby or career.

Happy hacking!

09.
Sample programs

In this section

Bat-and-ball game   **114**

Employee directory   **116**

Text editor   **118**

Headlines   **120**

Most of the code listings in this book have been short and snappy, so that you can learn about specific features and skills in Python without being distracted by unrelated fluff. You may, however, be eager to see some properly fleshed-out programs, so we've included a few here for you to study, modify and build upon.

All of these programs use the techniques covered in the book, but as complete examples, and with a few extra bits and pieces that we explain after the code. We hope they will inspire you to start writing your own apps, and feel free to take any code snippets and re-use them!

SAMPLE PROGRAMS
Bat-and-ball game

This is a simple game that elaborates upon the simple bouncing-ball demo we created in Listing 111. This time, however, we pep it up a bit by adding a bat along the bottom of the screen. Use the cursor keys to move the bat left and right, and try to keep the ball on the screen – this in turn keeps your score going up, which is shown in the top-left. If you miss the ball and it falls out of the bottom of the screen, it's game over!

```
1   import pygame, sys, random
2
3   pygame.init()
4
5   screen = pygame.display.set_mode((640, 480))
6
7   # Set up a new font
8   font = pygame.font.Font(None, 36)
9
10  score = 0
11
12  ball = pygame.image.load("ball.bmp")
13  ball_x = 10
14  ball_y = 10
15  ball_x_speed = 7
16  ball_y_speed = 7
17
18  bat = pygame.image.load("bat.bmp")
19  bat_x = 260
20  bat_y = 430
21
22  while 1:
23      for event in pygame.event.get():
24          if event.type == pygame.QUIT:
25              sys.exit()
```

```
26
27      score += 1
28
29      # Check for arrow key presses,
30      # and move bat accordingly
31      pressed = pygame.key.get_pressed()
32      if pressed[pygame.K_RIGHT] and bat_x < 512:
33          bat_x += 15
34      if pressed[pygame.K_LEFT] and bat_x > 0:
35          bat_x -= 15
36
37      ball_x += ball_x_speed
38      ball_y += ball_y_speed
39
40      # Collision detection code
41      if ball_x > bat_x and ball_x < bat_x + 112 and ↵
        ball_y > 400:
42          ball_y_speed = -(random.randint(5, 15))
43
44      if ball_x > 610: ball_x_speed = -(random. ↵
        randint(5, 15))
45      if ball_y > 450: break
46      if ball_x < 0: ball_x_speed = random.randint(5, 15)
47      if ball_y < 0: ball_y_speed = random.randint(5, 15)
48
49      screen.fill((240, 255, 255))
50
51      # Generate and render score text
52      scoretext = font.render("Score: " + str(score), 1, (30, 30, 30))
53      screen.blit(scoretext, (10, 10))
54
55      screen.blit(ball, (ball_x, ball_y))
56      screen.blit(bat, (bat_x, bat_y))
57
58      pygame.display.flip()
59      pygame.time.wait(10)
60
61  print("Your score was:", score)
```

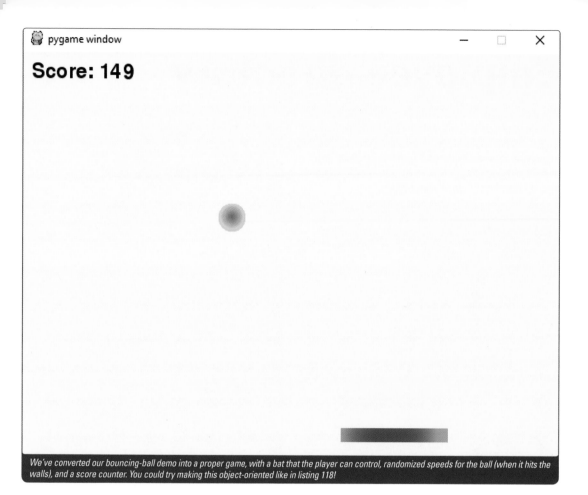

Score: 149

We've converted our bouncing-ball demo into a proper game, with a bat that the player can control, randomized speeds for the ball (when it hits the walls), and a score counter. You could try making this object-oriented like in listing 118!

There are a few things we've introduced here. On line 8, we set up a font with a point size of 36. Note that we set "None" as a name, which tells Pygame to use whatever is available (its default font). This is a good way to ensure that your games are completely multi-platform – i.e. they run on Windows, macOS and Linux without any problems. If you start trying to use system-specific fonts, you may run into difficulties later.

Lines 31 to 35 handle input from the user. We check to see if the user is pressing the left or right cursor keys, and then move the bat 15 pixels to the left or right respectively. But we also do a bit of checking to ensure that the bat can't be moved entirely off the screen. For a full list of keys you can scan for in Pygame, see **www.pygame.org/docs/ref/key.html**.

Lines 41 and 42 are responsible for collision detection; that is, seeing if the ball has hit the bat, and changing the ball's vertical speed to negative if so. Take a look at the code here, and you can see we check to see if the ball's position is around the top of the bat, bearing in mind that the ball is 32 pixels wide and the bat is 128. This collision detection code is very rudimentary and doesn't take into account the angle from where the ball is coming – but it does the job.

Also note the use of random numbers on lines 42, 44, 46 and 47 to generate the ball speeds. This is purely to make the game more interesting, as the player won't know how the ball is going to react off a wall! On lines 42 and 44 we generate negative speeds between -5 and -15, while on the other lines we generate positive speeds between 5 and 15. As with the bouncing ball demo, these are added on to the ball's position in each iteration of the main game loop.

On lines 52 and 53 we generate the score text string (including the contents of the "score" variable) and display it. Finally, once the game has been lost, we print the final score on the command line.

SAMPLE PROGRAMS
Employee directory

We've used the employee directory example a few times in this book – now it's time to create a complete program, using OOP, pickling, lists, data storage and many of the other techniques we explored. To run this program, you'll need to install the "Dill" module, so do that by entering this command first: "pip3 install dill".

```python
1   import sys, os
2   import dill as pickle
3
4   class Employee(object):
5       def __init__(self, passed_name, passed_number, ↵
        passed_comment):
6           self.name = passed_name
7           self.number = passed_number
8           self.comment = passed_comment
9
10      def find(self, search_term):
11          if self.name.lower().find(search_term. ↵
            lower()) != -1:
12              return 1
13          elif self.number.lower().find(search_term. ↵
            lower()) != -1:
14              return 1
15          elif self.comment.lower().find(search_term. ↵
            lower()) != -1:
16              return 1
17          else:
18              return 0
19
20      def show(self):
21          print("Name:", self.name)
22          print("Number:", self.number)
23          print("Comment:", self.comment)
24
25  def load_data(filename):
26      try:
27          global employees
28          file_data = open(filename, "rb")
29          employees = pickle.load(file_data)
30          input("\nData loaded - hit enter to continue...")
31          file_data.close()
32
33      except OSError as err:
34          print("File couldn't be opened:")
35          print(err)
36          sys.exit(1)
37
38  def save_data(filename):
39      try:
40          global employees
41          file_data = open(filename, "wb")
42          pickle.dump(employees, file_data)
43          file_data.close()
44          input("\nData saved - hit enter to continue...")
45
46      except OSError as err:
47          print("File couldn't be saved:")
48          print(err)
49          input("\nHit enter to continue...")
50
51  employees = []
52  choice = 0
53
54  if len(sys.argv) == 1:
55      print("No filename specified - starting with ↵
        empty data")
56      input("Hit enter to continue...")
57  else:
58      load_data(sys.argv[1])
59
60  while choice != 6:
61      if sys.platform == "win32":
62          os.system("cls")
63      else:
64          os.system("clear")
65
66      print("===== Employee Directory Manager ↵
        2.0 =====\n")
67      print(" 1. List employees")
68      print(" 2. Add employee")
69      print(" 3. Delete employee")
70      print(" 4. Search employees")
71      print(" 5. Save data")
72      print(" 6. Quit")
73
74      choice = int(input("\nEnter your choice: "))
75
76      if choice == 1:
77          for x in range(0, len(employees)):
78              print("\nEmployee number:", x + 1)
79              employees[x].show()
80          input("\nHit enter to continue...")
81
82      elif choice == 2:
83          name = input("\nEnter employee name: ")
84          number = input("Enter employee number: ")
85          comment = input("Enter employee comment: ")
86          employees.append(Employee(name, ↵
            number, comment))
```

```
87        input("\nEmployee added - hit enter to ↵
          continue...")
88
89     elif choice == 3:
90        number = int(input("\nEnter employee ↵
          number to remove: "))
91        if number > len(employees):
92           input ("No such employee! Hit enter to ↵
             continue...")
93        else:
94           del employees[number - 1]
95           input("\nEmployee removed - hit enter to ↵
             continue...")
96
97     elif choice == 4:
98        search_term = input("\nEnter a name, ↵
          number or comment: ")
99        for x in range(0, len(employees)):
100          result = employees[x].find(search_term)
101          if result == 1:
102             print("\nEmployee number:", x + 1)
103             employees[x].show()
104       input("\nHit enter to continue...")
105
106    elif choice == 5:
107       filename = input("\nEnter a filename: ")
108       save_data(filename)
```

The "Dill" module provides the same functionality as pickling, but is more flexible for storing classes and instances of objects. We import it on line 2, but using "as" we change how it's referred to in the program. This way we can use familiar "pickle.load" and "pickle.dump" routines, but the Dill versions will be used instead.

In this program, each employee is an object; the class definition contains three attributes, for the employee's name, number and a comment (any extra data that the program's user wants to add). In addition, each object has a "find" method, which takes a search parameter. If the search parameter is found anywhere in the employee's data, the method returns 1; otherwise it returns 0 (zero). There's also a "show" method, which simply displays the employee's details.

We define routines to load and save data using pickling, performing some checks and displaying prompts to hit the enter key (the "input" routine is ideal for this – we can just discard the data it returns). Then we set up our "employees" list, which will be a list of class instances, and start a main loop. The program clears the screen according to the operating system on which it's running, then displays a menu and responds to selections accordingly.

Look at lines 76 to 80: we set up a loop that iterates through every object in the list, and call its "show" method. To the user, employee numbers start from 1 (hence the "+ 1" in line 78), but we know internally Python lists begin from zero. The rest of the program should be fairly straightforward – so why not try modifying it? You could add a menu item and a chunk of code to modify an existing employee, asking for an employee number and then asking for updated details. Or you could add another menu item that offers to display a specific range of employees, e.g. starting with 5 and ending with 10.

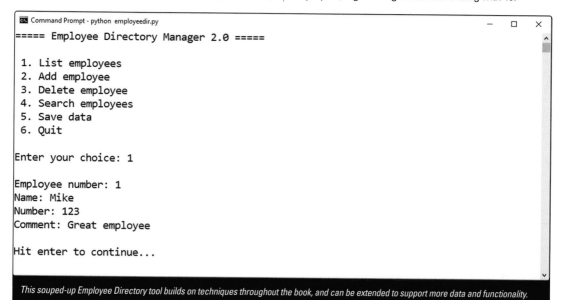

```
Command Prompt - python employeedir.py                    —    □    ×
===== Employee Directory Manager 2.0 =====

1. List employees
2. Add employee
3. Delete employee
4. Search employees
5. Save data
6. Quit

Enter your choice: 1

Employee number: 1
Name: Mike
Number: 123
Comment: Great employee

Hit enter to continue...
```

This souped-up Employee Directory tool builds on techniques throughout the book, and can be extended to support more data and functionality.

SAMPLE PROGRAMS
Text editor

As you may have guessed from the name, this is a text editor. Yes, thanks to Tkinter we can implement a usable editor, with file loading and saving facilities, a clickable menu and other features, all in just 43 lines of code (or even fewer if you remove the blanks that we added for cosmetic reasons).

To do this, we add some extras from Tkinter: "scrolledtext" provides a rectangular widget for editing plain text (including scrollbars where necessary); "filedialog" lets us create file open and save dialogs; and "messagebox" is used for pop-up messages (like an "About" dialog). Here's the code:

```
1   from tkinter import *
2   from tkinter import scrolledtext
3   from tkinter import filedialog
4   from tkinter import messagebox
5   import sys
6
7   def open_file():
8       file = filedialog.askopenfile(mode = "r")
9       if file != None:
10          text.delete("1.0", END)
11          text.insert("1.0", file.read())
12          file.close()
13
14  def save_file():
15      file = filedialog.asksaveasfile(mode = "w")
16      if file != None:
17          file.write(text.get("1.0", END))
18          file.close()
19
20  def about_dialog():
21      messagebox.showinfo("About", "Version 1.0\nEnjoy!")
22
23  def exit_app():
24      sys.exit(0)
25
26  root_win = Tk()
27  root_win.title("Text Editor")
28  root_win.geometry("640x480")
29
30  main_menu = Menu(root_win)
31  root_win.config(menu = main_menu)
32
33  file_menu = Menu(main_menu)
34  main_menu.add_cascade(label="File", menu =
    file_menu)
35  file_menu.add_command(label="Open",
    command = open_file)
36  file_menu.add_command(label="Save",
    command = save_file)
37  file_menu.add_command(label="About",
    command = about_dialog)
38  file_menu.add_command(label="Exit",
    command = exit_app)
39
40  text = scrolledtext.ScrolledText(root_win,
    width = 80, height = 30)
41  text.pack(fill = "both", expand = "yes")
42
43  root_win.mainloop()
```

Let's start from line 26, where execution begins: we create a new root window and set its size and dimensions accordingly. On lines 30 and 31, we create a new menu and apply it to the root window. This is just an empty menu bar at the moment, so on lines 33 and 34 we create a new item in the menu bar – a "File" menu. Then, from lines 35 to 38, we add entries to this "File" menu, using the "command" parameters to link the menu entries to functions that we defined earlier in the file.

Line 40 creates a new text entry widget inside our root window, while line 41 packs it into the root window, saying that it should fill the window and expand if the user resizes the window. So we end up with a text entry box that fills up the whole window – apart from the menu bar at the top on Windows and most Linux distributions, of course.

Now we can look at the functions linked to the menu items: on line 8 we pop up a dialog and ask the user to pick a file to open; we can then access this file, our "file" object. If opening the file succeeds, we want to delete any existing content in the text entry widget before adding in the new text – so that's what we do on line 10. The "1.0" here refers to the first line and the first character of the text widget's content, meaning we have another silly numbering system

to learn! Yes, in Tkinter parlance, lines count from 1 and characters on the lines count from zero. You just have to get used to it...

So on line 10, we delete from the very start of the file to "END", which is a special keyword meaning the end of the file. Then on line 11 we insert the contents of the file at the start of the text area. For saving files, the process is similar; from line 14 onwards we pop up a dialog for choosing a filename to save to, and then use "text.get" with the start and end of the data to get all text from the entry widget and write it to the file.

On line 21 for the "About" menu entry we pop up a simple dialog box with two parameters: a title, and the text to be displayed. Note that we can use the "\n" newline character to break up the lines inside the dialog box.

And that's it! We've looked at some more features of Tkinter here, so once you've explored this program and want to write more graphical apps, head over to **https://wiki.python.org/moin/TkInter** for a detailed list of resources, tips and guides.

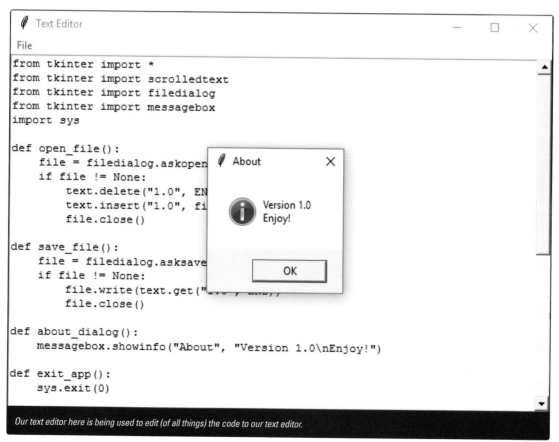

Our text editor here is being used to edit (of all things) the code to our text editor.

SAMPLE PROGRAMS
Headlines

Our final program demonstrates how to retrieve and parse information from the internet. Back in Listing 105, we created a very rudimentary web "browser" that pulled HTML data from a web server and displayed it on the screen – but we didn't do anything with the data itself. We essentially just retrieved a bunch of bytes and printed them.

This time, we're going to process the data we receive into a more readable form. To achieve this, we're going to get a bunch of headlines from the popular Reddit discussion website, where users post links to articles and then engage in discussions about them. First of all, if you've never been to Reddit before, visit **https://www.reddit.com/r/worldnews/** to get an idea of what it's like – you'll see a list of headlines about world news events, which link through to articles on various websites. Underneath each headline you'll see a link to comments, where Reddit users discuss the news.

Along with the "worldnews" section of Reddit (a section is also known as a "subreddit"), there are other sections as well. For instance, **https://www.reddit.com/r/unitedkingdom/** is for articles and discussions about the UK, while **https://www.reddit.com/r/python/** covers the Python programming language.

Now, we're going to write a program that extracts a bunch of headlines from a subreddit and displays them, updating the headlines every 60 seconds in case new ones have been posted. If you have a multiple monitor setup, you could put a window running this program in the corner of your display, so that you can keep track of events while going about your work. Or if you're feeling especially ambitious, you could set up a Raspberry Pi with a small LCD display that shows the headlines.

If you go to the "worldnews" subreddit in your web browser and view the HTML source code, you'll see that it's mightily complicated – so how can we extract the headlines from all that? The solution is to use the RSS "feed", or data, from that subreddit. RSS (Rich Site Summary) is a data format based on XML that contains just the essentials of a web page, and it's much easier to work with than giant mixtures of HTML, CSS and JavaScript.

You can see what RSS looks like: go to **https://www.reddit.com/r/worldnews/.rss** (note the ".rss" at the end) in your browser and view the source again. It's all on one line, so you'll have to scroll around a bit, but you can see that it's considerably simpler. Most

importantly, it contains elements that we can pick out for our headline-displaying program: titles and links.

So here's the program. To parse RSS we need the "feedparser" module, so install it with "pip3 install feedparser" beforehand.

```
1   import feedparser, time
2   import sys, os
3
4   subreddit = input("\nEnter the subreddit (eg ↵
    'worldnews') to view: ")
5   no_of_items = int(input("How many headlines ↵
    do you want to show? "))
6   show_urls = input("Show URLs as well? y/n: ")
7   filter = input("Enter a word or term you want to ↵
    filter out: ")
8
9   while 1:
10      if sys.platform == "win32":
11          os.system("cls")
12      else:
13          os.system("clear")
14
15      myfeed = feedparser.parse ↵
        ("https://www.reddit.com/r/" + subreddit \
16          + "/.rss")
17
18      if len(myfeed["entries"]) == 0:
19          print("Subreddit not valid!")
20          sys.exit(1)
21
22      x = 1
23
24      for post in myfeed.entries:
25          if len(filter) > 0:
26              if post.title.lower().find(filter.lower()) == -1:
27                  print("* " + post.title)
28                  if show_urls == "y":
29                      print("  (" + post.link + ")")
30          else:
31              print("* " + post.title)
32              if show_urls == "y":
33                  print("  (" + post.link + ")")
34          x += 1
35          if x > no_of_items:
36              break
37
38      time.sleep(60)
```

After importing the modules we need, we ask the user a few questions on lines 4 to 7. The "filter" part asks for a word or term that should be filtered out – so headlines containing that text will not be displayed.

On line 9 we set up an infinite loop, and then on lines 10 to 13 we clear the screen using OS-specific routines, as we explored earlier. Lines 15 and 16 are actually part of the same line of code, but broken up using a backslash character for better formatting in this book. These lines do the crucial work: they tell the "feedparser" Python module to retrieve the RSS data for the subreddit specified by the user, which is then stored in our "myfeed" object. If the user has entered a non-existing or empty subreddit, however, there will be no items in "myfeed", so we should quit out – and that's exactly what we check for on lines 18 to 20.

Line 22 sets up a temporary counter variable called "x", which we use to make sure we're only showing the number of headlines that the user entered on line 5. (Reddit's RSS feeds contain a maximum of 25 headlines, so if the user enters a higher number it won't have an effect.) We increment this "x" variable as we process each headline, and finish displaying when "x" is greater than the "no_of_items" value that the user entered.

Lines 24 to 36 set up a loop with multiple levels of indentation. This loop goes through every Reddit post (message) in the "myfeed" data, and then gets the headline ("post.title") and link ("post.link"). We check to see if the user entered a word to filter out on line 25, and if so, we check to see if the headline contains that word on line 26. If not, we display the headline, and optionally the link as well in brackets underneath.

The indented code from line 31 to 33 is executed if the user didn't enter any filter word(s). Finally, on line 38 we make the program pause for a minute, before the next iteration of the infinite loop on line 9 starts and an updated set of headlines is retrieved from the subreddit.

Many websites offer RSS feeds, so you can customize this program to pull all sorts of data from the internet, parse it and display it in different ways. You could make a weather app, for instance, or access sports data and show results. Try searching the web for "weather RSS" or "sports RSS" to find some feeds, and for more information about the "feedparser" module, see the documentation at **https://pythonhosted.org/feedparser/**.

Challenge answers

SECTION 02
1 They must start with a letter and not use existing function or keyword names
2 "b = int(a)"
3 A number with decimal points, e.g. 1.234
4 "a += 5"
5 25; it multiplies 5 by 3, and then adds the result on to 10. To get the other result of 45, use "(10 + 5) * 3" so that the addition is done first

SECTION 03
1 "if a == 2" – the double equals signs mean comparison. A single sign mean assignment
2 Spaces are preferred by most Python coders (e.g. four spaces for each level of indentation), but it doesn't matter. The main thing is to be consistent!
3 If "a" is less than or equal to 5
4 ".lower()"
5 "break"

SECTION 04
1 At the beginning, so that Python knows they exist before your main code tries to call them
2 They contain parameters – data passed to the functions. This data is then accessible as variables inside the function
3 "def test(a = 10)"
4 "return"
5 Local variables are only accessible inside the function in which they were created; global variables can be accessed in other functions and in the main code

SECTION 05
1 "mystring[4]" – remember that we count from zero when going through elements!
2 Tuples are defined with round brackets and their contents can't be changed; lists are defined with square brackets and their contents can be changed
3 "mylist.sort(key=str.lower)"
4 'del employees["Bob"]'
5 "def summary(*data):"

SECTION 06
1 "\n"
2 "wb"
3 "seek(offset)"
4 0 to 65535, inclusive
5 Import the "sys" module and it will be in "sys.argv[1]"

SECTION 07
1 Import the "sys" module and check "sys.platform" – it's "win32" for Windows, "linux" for Linux, and "darwin" for macOS
2 Import the "os" module and do 'os.system("test.exe")'
3 Import the "random" module and use "random. randint(20, 90)"
4 Execute "display.flip()"
5 Place the variables and function definitions in a separate file, e.g. "mymodule.py", and then use "import mymodule" in your main code file

SECTION 08
1 A method
2 In good coding practice, all class names start with capital letters
3 It is always called whenever a new instance of a class is created
4 A method that is automatically called whenever a certain attribute is set/changed
5 A variable shared between all instances of the class

Glossary

append To add something, usually to a piece of writing.

argument A value passed to a function or method when calling it.

binary Relating to or involving a method of calculating and of representing information in computers by using the numbers 0 and 1. Also, consisting of two things or parts.

byte A unit of computer information that is equal to eight bits.

elif A coding statement short for "else if."

endianness Refers to the order in which bytes are arranged or organized when stored in memory on computers or when transmitted over digital links.

enumerate To name things one after another in a list, or to count.

function A series of statements which returns some value to a caller and helps separate code into useful parts.

integer Any whole number, or number that is not a fraction or decimal.

iteration The action of repeating, such as the repetition of a sequence of computer instructions a specified number of times or until a condition is met.

lucrative Profitable.

module A part of Python code that's kept in a separate file.

parameter A named part within a function or method definition that specifies an argument (or arguments) that the function is able to accept.

supersede To take the place of something (usually something no longer useful).

tuple A sequence of immutable Python objects, similar to lists. However, unlike lists, tuples cannot be changed and use parentheses rather than brackets.

variable A quantity that can have any one of a set of values or a symbol that represents such a quantity.

venerable Old and respected.

verbatim In exactly the same words.

For More Information

Girls Who Code
28 West 23rd Street, 4th Floor
New York, NY 10010
Website: http://www.girlswhocode.com
Facebook and Twitter: @GirlsWhoCode
YouTube: Girls Who Code
The aim of Girls Who Code is to interest young women in computer programming as a career and to give them skills and resources to become involved and succeed in the field.

IEEE Computer Society
2001 L Street NW, Suite 700
Washington, DC 20036-4928
(800) 272-6657
Facebook: @ieeecomputersociety
Twitter: @ComputerSociety
YouTube: ieeeComputerSociety
Website: http://www.computer.org
The IEEE Computer Society is a good place to find information on many different aspects of technology. It sponsors conferences, as well as other learning opportunities, and offers student memberships.

National Association of Programmers (NAP)
P.O. Box 529
Prairieville, LA 70769
Website: http://napusa.org
The NAP is a national group promoting the work of programmers. It offers resources to both professionals and students in the field and sponsors various events.

Python Software Foundation (PSF)
9450 SW Gemini Drive
ECM# 90772
Beaverton, OR 97008
Website: http://python.org/psf
Twitter: @ThePSF
The PSF promotes and develops the Python programming language and works hard to support Python programmers around the world.

For Further Reading

Briggs, Jason R. *Python for Kids: A Playful Introduction to Programming*. San Francisco, CA: No Starch Press, 2013.

Donat, Wolfram. *Learn Raspberry Pi Programming with Python*. New York, NY: Apress, 2014.

Gonzales, Andrea, and Sophie Houser. *Girl Code: Gaming, Going Viral, and Getting It Done*. New York, NY: Harper, an imprint of HarperCollinsPublishers, 2017.

Grantham, Sway. *Raspberry Pi Projects Workbook*. New York, NY: DK, 2017.

Harbour, Jonathan S. *Video Game Programming for Kids*. Boston, MA: Course Technology, 2013.

Harrison, Matt. *Treading on Python, Volume 1: Foundations of Python*. Seattle, WA: CreateSpace, 2012.

Harrison, Matt. *Treading on Python, Volume 2: Intermediate Python*. Seattle, WA: CreateSpace, 2013.

Kalb, Irv. *Learn to Program with Python*. Berkeley, CA: Apress, 2016.

Keranen, Rachel. *The Power of Python*. New York, NY: Cavendish Square Publishing, 2018.

Lambert, Kenneth A. *Python Programming for Teens*. Boston, MA: Cengage Learning PTR, 2015.

LEAD Project. *Super Scratch Programming Adventure! Learn to Program by Making Cool Games*. San Francisco, CA: No Starch Press, 2012.

Monk, Simon. *Programming the Raspberry Pi: Getting Started with Python*. New York, NY: McGraw-Hill, 2013.

Richardson, Matt, and Shawn Wallace. *Getting Started with Raspberry Pi*. Sebastopol, CA: Maker Media, 2013.

Sande, Warren, and Carter Sande. *Hello World! Computer Programming for Kids and Other Beginners*. 2nd ed. Greenwich, CT: Manning Publications, 2013.

Steele, Craig, and Carol Vorderman MBE, Dr. Claire Quigley, Dr. Martin Goodfellow, Daniel McCafferty, Dr. Jon Woodcock. *Coding Projects in Python*. New York, NY: DK Penguin Random House, 2017.

Sweigart, Al. *Making Games with Python and Pygame: A Guide to Programming with Graphics, Animation, and Sound*. Seattle, WA: CreateSpace, 2012.

Young Rewired State. *Get Coding! Learn HTML, CSS, and JavaScript and Build a Website, App, and Game*. Somerville, MA: Candlewick Press, 2017.

Index

administrator 73
Amiga OS 90
and (operator) 35
Android 10
append (file) 74
append (lists) *see* data
ASCII text 17
assignment 22-23, 25

bat and ball game 114
binary numbers *see* data
blank lines in code 32
buttons 99-101
byte 77, 80-81

case-insensitive string sort 62
cat (command) 73
cd (command) 16, 17
chr (function) 52
circle, area of 91, 99
classes 105-111
    attributes 106-111, 117
    base 109
    definition 105, 117
    generic 111
    get 107
    inheritance 109-110
    init 105
    instances 105
    logic 107-109
    methods 37, 105-111
    objects 72, 97, 105-111, 117, 119
    self 106
    set 107
    slots 110-111
    subclasses 109
    variables 106
        private 107
clear/cls (command) 90
close (file) 72, 74
code block 33
Code Club 6

collision detection 115
command line (prompt) 12, 14, 15, 16,
    17, 78
    parameters (arguments) 78
commenting 28
comparisons 32-37
    case insensitive 37
    chaining 35
    equal to 34
    less than 34
    more than 34
    multiple 33
    not equal to 34
conditional statements *see*
    comparisons *and* if
CPU (central processing unit) 7
CSS (Cascading Style Sheets)
    93, 120
CSV (comma separated value) 76, 77

Darwin (macOS) 89
data 56-85
    binary numbers 77-78, 80
    dictionaries 63-66, 76, 82
        keys 64
        mixed data 64
        object-specific 111
        values 64
    elements 40, 56-57, 60
        changing 61
        position in 80
        sorting, adding & removing
            62-63
    handling 82-85
    JSON format 83-85
    lists 39-40, 60-63, 92, 108, 116
        append 62
        comprehension 85
        elements 40, 61-63
        sublists 60, 62
        unpacking 69
    offset 80
    open (load) 72, 75-75

ord 78
parse 77, 78, 82
pickling 82, 116
    dump routine 82, 117
    load routine 82, 117
read 75, 80
read binary 77-78
readlines 75
read-only mode 75, 80
searching through 79-81
    ignore case 79
seek 80
slices 59, 60-61
split 76
storage 116
structured data 76
structures 56-57
tuples 57-59, 67, 69, 92
    elements 61
    immutable 60
    unpacking 69
    words 81
write (save) 72-74, 83
date and time (current) 91
dictionaries *see* data
Dill (module) *see* modules

education, coding in 6
elements *see* data
elif 35-37, 65
else 35-37
Emacs text editor 17
embedded devices 88
employee directory program 116
end (print parameter) 52, 75
enumerate (function) 61-62, 79
equals sign 22
error messages 17
    attribute error 111
    file errors 73
    permission denied 73
    recursion error 46
events 98

exception handling 73, 75
exec (function) 51-52
extend (lists) 62

filedialog (Tkinter) 118-119
filenames 78, 82
  split 95
Finder (mac) 16
flip routine 97
floating-point numbers 27, 53
flowchart 34, 36, 38
fonts 115
for loop see loops
functions 25, 27, 44-53
  calling (executing) 44
  creating (defining) 44
  feeding results 28
  infinite recursion 47
  multiple 45

gigabyte 77
GUI (graphical user interface)
  applications 99-101
  PyQt 101
  PySide 101
  Tkinter 99-101
  toolkit ideas 101
  wxPython 101

hash symbol 28
headlines program 120
"Hello, world!" 20
HTML (Hypertext Markup Language)
  85, 93, 120-121

IDEs (Integrated Development
  Environments), list of 101
if (comparison) 32-37, 58, 65
  nested 33
image manipulation 95
import (modules) see modules
indentation 33, 83
  tabs vs spaces 33
index (lists) 63
init see classes
input 25-28

insert (lists) 62
instances see classes
integer (int) 27, 28, 76
items (dictionaries) 66

Javascript 82, 120
JPEG file format 95

kilobyte 77

label see Tkinter
len (function) 53
Linux 10, 11, 89
  forums 14
  installing Python on 12
lists see data
load see data
loops 38-40, 45
  breaking out 39
  for 39-40, 58, 59, 61, 63, 66, 75,
    76, 77, 85
  infinite 39, 98, 120-121
  range 40
  while 38-39

macOS 10, 11, 15
  command line 16
  installing Python on 12
make plain text (text editor) 16
malware 73
math (module) see modules
math operators 24-25
  precedence 24
  shorthand 25
megabyte 77
memory 22, 56
messagebox (Tkinter) 118-119
methods see classes
modularity 44, 46, 50, 66, 104, 106
modules 6, 88-101
  creating 94
  Dill 116-117
  documentation (general) 89
  feedparser 120-121
    documentation 121
  importing 78, 82, 83

managing 95
math 91, 100
  documentation 91
os 90
  documentation 90
Pillow (PIL) 95
  documentation 96
Pygame 96-99, 115
random 91-92
  documentation 92
socket 93
sys 78, 88
  documentation 89
time 91
Tkinter 99-101, 118-119
  documentation 101, 119
Untangle 85
  documentation 85
modulo operation 39

Nano text editor 17
NetBSD 93
network programming 93
network protocols 94
new line character 65-66, 74, 75-76,
  119
Notepad text editor 15, 16
Notepad++ text editor 17

object-oriented programming (OOP)
  104, 116
objects see classes
offset see data
open (file) see data
open-source software 10
operating system 11, 15, 20, 78
or (operator) 35
ord (data) see data
OSError see exception handling
os (module) see modules

pack see Tkinter
parameters 21, 23
  arbitrary number of 67
  default 48
  multiple 47-48
  passing 47-49, 105
PATH, add Python 3.x to 12
pickling see data
pillow (module) see modules

Pip module manager 95
plain text editor 15
point-and-click apps 99
pop (lists) 63
ports (network) 93
pow (function) 53
print 20-21 and throughout
    parameters 26
processors 38
Pygame (module) *see* modules
Python
    2.7 (version) 12
    3 (version) 11, 12
    community resources 125
    installing 11-14
        Linux 12
        macOS 12
        Raspberry Pi 14
        Windows 11
    interpreter 20, 37, 45
    license 10
    release level 89
    setting up 10-17
    Style Guide for Code 33
    version number 89
    why choose 6
    writing and running programs 15

random (module) *see* modules
random numbers 92
range 40
Raspberry Pi 6, 120
    command line 17
    installing Python on 14
Raspbian OS 14
raw text 16
read access 17
read (file) *see* data
Reddit (website) 120-121
remainder 39
remove excess data 76
repetition 38-40
return (data) 49, 67
RGB color values 97
Rich Text Format 17

root user 73
root window *see* Tkinter
round (function) 53
RSS (Rich Site Summary) 120-121
    parsing 120-121

save (file) *see* data
scrolledtext (Tkinter) 118-119
seek *see* data
sleep routine 91
slices *see* data
SlickEdit text editor 17
slots *see* classes
Socket (module) *see* modules
source code (Python) 20
spaces (indentation) 33
split (data) *see* data
Spotlight (mac) 16
spreadsheet 76
SSH 17
storage media 72
strftime (string formatted time) 91
strings 21, 23, 26, 57
    literal 23
    naming rules 23
    variable 23
StringVar routine (Tkinter) 100
stub function 65
Sublime Text editor 17
sys (module) *see* modules

tab separated files 77 *see also*
    CSV
tabs (indentation) 33
Terminal 12
text editor 15-17
    advanced features 17
    auto-completion 17
    Python program 118-119
    syntax highlighting 17
text entry box (Tkinter) 118-119
TextEdit 16
time (module) *see* modules
Tkinter (module) *see* modules

trigonometric functions 91 *see also*
    math (module)
try *see* exception handling
tuples *see* data
type (command) 73

Unicode standard 52
Untangle (module) *see* modules

variables 22-23 and throughout
    assignment 22-23, 25
    class 106
    global 50-51
    list 39-40
    local 50-51, 105
    numerical 24, 26
    scope 50-51
    string 24, 26
video game development 96
    Pygame *see* modules
Vim text editor 17

web browser 93
web editor 15
web server 120-121
while loop 38-39, 65
windows *see* GUI
Windows (Microsoft) 11, 15, 89
    explorer 11
    installing Python on 11
with (keyword) 74
words (data) *see* data
word processor 15
write (file) *see* data

XML (Extensible Markup Language)
    85
    convert to Python data object 85
XTerm 12

ZX Spectrum (Sinclair) 72